MW00587221

PRAISE FOR THRIVING AFTER BURNOUT

Dr. Jennifer Johnson provides strategies and care tasks to enhance your life professionally and personally. Learn positive ways to take care of yourself allowing you to thrive the way you want. Live fully into your humanness.

— EVAN ROBB, EDUCATOR, AUTHOR, SPEAKER

This is the first book to make me feel seen - floating, hopeful mess and all. It is *real*. It's not one of those overly positive keynote speeches where you roll your eyes at your teacher friend. It's instead one of those professional developments where the speaker comes in, takes their shoes off, speaks to you like a human, and gives you something you can use that day. This book gives us what we actually need to heal our souls and keep us going in the classroom (or whatever the education world looks like for you).

— JESSICA ALSIP, DEAF EDUCATION TEACHER, IRVING, TEXAS

As a school superintendent, Dr. Johnson's book has given me the tools necessary to begin to recover from my own burnout. Using real world examples, this brilliant 'how to' guide is revolutionary for anyone in the field of education and beyond. During these tumultuous times, Dr. Johnson has given us a gift, with an easy step-by-step road map with realistic daily strategies to help to manage one's stress levels; thus halting the cycle of burnout."

— DR. MICHELLE ROSENBERG, SCHOOL SUPERINTENDENT, NEW JERSEY

Dr. Johnson is authentic and inspiring. She writes with a profound and approachable voice, offering readers an uplifting, supportive book full of strategies and practices that will help you thrive after burnout.

— JENNIFER ABRAMS, EDUCATIONAL
CONSULTANT AND AUTHOR OF *HAVING HARD
CONVERSATIONS*

THRIVing After Burnout is a beneficial read for all educators from first year teachers to seasoned veterans and support staff. The book is written in brief sections providing well-researched strategies for easy implementation. I'm excited about trying out these ideas presented by Dr. Johnson.

— JOY FOWLER, 1ST GRADE TEACHER, 35 YEARS
OF SERVICE

Teachers of the deaf/hard of hearing frequently find themselves fighting for the rights of their students to an equitable education. Along the way, burnout all too often becomes a way of life. Dr. Johnson's book is a breath of fresh air in its compassionate approach to unraveling the cause of burnout, and strategies to feel more effective and successful. After living through our recent pandemic, we ALL need to know healthy responses to burnout!

— KAREN L. ANDERSON, PH.D., DIRECTOR,
SUPPORTING SUCCESS FOR CHILDREN WITH
HEARING LOSS

Now more than ever, those who serve in public schools are facing never ending challenges that are stressful to the physical, mental, and spiritual health of the individual. Dr. Johnson provides a succinct guide filled with evidence-based solutions to address the realities of balancing the demands of work, family and most importantly self for all educators. "THRIVing After Burnout" is a must read, and will not only benefit the educators, but the students and their families that they serve as well.

— CARIN RENEE SHEARER PH.D., BCBA, LBA,
DIRECTOR OF SPECIAL EDUCATION
LEWISVILLE, TEXAS

Dr. Johnson communicates practical and useful strategies for educators who are struggling in today's world of education, with a sincere and personal touch.

— RUTH E DUBNER, M.ED., LPC-S, NCC,
LICENSED PROFESSIONAL COUNSELOR IN
SCHOOLS

Whether you're working to recover from burnout or striving to avoid it, Jennifer brings solid, research-based, practical suggestions to this great resource for educators. And, through her heartfelt sharing of her own struggles, she brings hope to readers that they, too, will be able to bring their best selves to school, day in and day out.

— JANE KISE, ED.D., DIFFERENTIATED
COACHING ASSOCIATES

Once I picked up "Thriving After Burnout: A Teacher's Compassionate Guide," I couldn't put it down until I was finished. I have personally either witnessed or experienced everything Dr. Johnson addresses in this book. After an extremely difficult past few years, I am so excited to put these strategies into practice and reignite my passion for working with students!

— REBECCA ATKINSON, PH.D., LICENSED
SPECIALIST IN SCHOOL PSYCHOLOGY, FRISCO,
TEXAS

Dr. Jen gives realistic strategies that can be implemented immediately. She's been in the trenches and gives easy to follow step by step instruction on how to dig yourself out. A must have, not just for teachers, but for anyone seeking to improve their lives.

— KRISTI BRASHIER, M.S., SCHOOL-BASED
SPEECH LANGUAGE PATHOLOGIST

THRIVING AFTER BURNOUT

A Teacher's Compassionate Guide

JEN JOHNSON, PHD

Copyright © 2022 by Jennifer A. L. Johnson, Ph.D.

All rights reserved.

No part of this book may be reproduced in any form or means. Any unauthorized use, sharing, reproduction or distribution of these materials by any means, electronic, mechanical or otherwise is strictly prohibited. No portion of these materials may be reproduced in any manner whatsoever, without the express written consent of the publisher, except for the use of brief quotations in a book review.

Red Thread Publishing LLC. 2022

Write to info@redthreadbooks.com if you are interested in publishing with Red Thread Publishing. Learn more about publications or foreign rights acquisitions of our catalog of books: www.redthreadbooks.com

Paperback ISBN: 9781955683272

Ebook ISBN: 9781955683289

Cover Design: Vanessa Goez

Author Photo © Brad Barton

CONTENTS

Dedicated to YOU, dear friend.

PREFACE

Recently, I interacted with a teacher on social media who was lamenting that her attendance was tied to her opportunity for advancement due to merit-based pay. While I was aware of merit-based systems, I wasn't aware that taking the allotted number of sick days per year impacted teacher pay in these systems.

At the time, I was writing a chapter in this book about taking sick days, and I realized that this might be important information to be aware of as I wrote strategies, so I asked a clarifying question, sharing that I was writing this book and interested in her perspective. Shortly after, an administrator commented that it wasn't this way everywhere. She asked what I could do to be a "friend to Texas public schools" and highlight the good that was happening, noting that there was already "enough pressure on the system."

In that moment, my brain raced with thoughts and emotions and analysis.

This administrator wasn't a random person. I know her. We worked together years ago when I was a teacher in K-12. I've watched her over the years climb the educational administration ladder and now she's an executive director. And I've not only watched her climb, but I've watched her climb well. I've watched her develop an organizational culture that I would put up against any award-winning school or system, and if I ever went back to public schools, I'd want to work for her.

So when I read that comment, it was a real gut punch.

What about my work and this book was not indicative of "friendly?" I wondered. What is more friendly than helping teachers learn and implement strategies that improve their emotional health so they can remain teachers in the system?

I stewed on this for days. I talked to those closest to me personally and professionally. I reached out to former and current clients. I asked them, "What does it mean to be a friend to public schools? What am I missing? What has gone wrong in my messaging?" I got two sets of answers, and those two sets opened my eyes to the underbelly of what happened that afternoon.

About half of the people I reached out to said that to be a friend of public schools meant you were a helper of some kind. You helped and supported where it was needed. They affirmed that I was, indeed, a friend of public schools in their minds because I was helping teachers stay in the classroom and become more emotionally healthy. I appreciated their affirmation, but it didn't really help me understand what it was that was prompting an insinuation that I wasn't a "friend" of public schools.

The other half were very straightforward when they shared that they were not surprised that some did not consider me a "friend" of public schools. One leader in particular stated that by empowering the small players in any system to honor their humanity, set boundaries, and require dignity from the system, I was becoming an enemy of the system. That hit really deep, and I've continued to think about how to reach folks who see my work as aversive.

I want to share with you some insights I learned as I explored this interaction that I think set the tone and intention of this book.

THE CRACKS IN THE FOUNDATION ARE SHOWING

I consider free and appropriate public education to be one of the hallmarks and greatest accomplishments of the United States of America. What we, as a field, have been able to achieve using shrinking public funding and support is something to be incredibly proud of.

When I studied the history of public schooling in my doctoral program, I remember literally ugly crying in my office at the University of North Texas reading "Being Heumann" by Judith Heumann as she described being able to attend public school for the first time as a child with a disability. We have served and continue to serve children in ways that other countries in the world do not.

Being a "worker" in the public school system has become more and more difficult over the years as expectations have changed, funding has either declined or remained stagnant, technology has rapidly developed, and the emotional health of children has increasingly become a priority due to collective trauma.

The world around us has rapidly morphed in the past 20 years, and we have struggled to keep up - not because we don't want to, but because the change that has occurred is complex, and complex changes require complex solutions, and complex solutions require trial, error, iteration, development, and time to curate.

THE SYSTEM IS BAD - *NOT* THE PEOPLE

I see administrators, like my former colleague, doing everything they can to support the development of the system - truly dedicating their entire careers and frankly, their lives, to improving public schools. When you pour your heart and soul into developing a system that is under extreme pressure, it is difficult to simultaneously process the pain of the people who are still being harmed in that system. Sometimes when you're the person trying to keep the ship afloat, it feels like an accusation or a personal attack when anyone points out another crack in the hull. Every criticism or critique, regardless of how accurate, is met with an automatic response of defensiveness, because you're working so hard where you are to change things.

I see you, admins! I see the fantastic work many of you are doing to change the culture. There are fantastic superintendents, principals, coordinators, and directors all over this country. There are great places to be a teacher where administrators have truly transformed their schools to be places where teachers can be human beings, and not robots.

But to focus solely on those individual places and people, and not on the problems in the system as a whole, is to bypass the harm that is being done to actual human beings and to gaslight teachers who really want to stay in education and are holding on by a thread.

WHAT THIS BOOK IS AND ISN'T

This book is not a celebration of all of the good things happening in public schools, though there are good things. This book is not a bashing of all of the bad things happening in public schools, though there are things we could discuss. I want to leave the celebration and bashing to those whose agenda it serves to do so.

My agenda is not to build up or break down the system. My agenda is to build up the people who work in the system. The teachers. The administrators. The instructional coaches. The paraprofessionals. The bus drivers. All educators.

This book is a collection of stories and evidence-based strategies that will resonate with the hearts of educators who are working in a system that has not been completely healed from the wounds of a worldwide pandemic.

It is a collection of stories where we will see the pain and hardships that arise from working in a system that has historically undervalued its greatest assets: the humans who keep it afloat.

This book is a collection of strategies to bring hope, energy, and connection to the teacher that desperately wants to stay in the class-room, but knows they are currently putting their mental and emotional health on the line to do so.

This book is a collection of strategies administrators can offer teachers as part of their efforts to provide an emotionally safe work environment where both students *and* teachers are able to thrive.

This book is a labor of deep love for a system that is worth saving, and that needs to be nurtured and supported through the integration of compassionate, human practices.

This book is a love letter to every educator in schools, public or otherwise, that I endearingly refer to as "friend."

AUTHOR'S NOTE

As I'm writing this, educators have completed teaching in the third year of a worldwide pandemic.

When it first started, I really didn't fully grasp what it would mean for educators or what the future would look like. In Spring of 2020, I was teaching at the University of North Texas and I was so hopeful this was just a weird blip that would resolve quickly and have short-term impacts.

K-12 teachers had such high hopes too. I heard teachers say, "If I can just get through the Spring of 2020, I'll be home free. It's hard, but it's just a couple of months."

And then Fall 2020 happened and Spring of 2021.

Virtual school, hybrid models, high-risk in-person learning environments. You thought it couldn't get worse.

And then it did.

The 2021-2022 school year brought new pressures, and many teachers reported it was even worse than the previous year.

Tanks empty.

Exhausted.

Fatigued.

Emotionally spent.

Underappreciated.

Underpaid.

Angry.

Sad.

Afraid.

BURNED OUT!

Burnout is a term we've used nonchalantly in education for decades. When I was a teacher, I remember lamenting, "I'm so burned out. I can't wait for Spring Break." We were tired and under-resourced and frustrated, but wow, the "burnout" then and the "burnout" now are two different animals, eh?

Back then, we wore "burnout" as a badge of honor, showing how dedicated we were to the profession (which wasn't healthy then either, by the way). Now it's worn by practically everyone, and it has nothing to do with how great a teacher you are, or how long you've been teaching, or how much you love kids. It almost seems inevitable!

Now, I know what you're thinking: this book is a real treat so far! Very encouraging, and you already feel better about the situation you're in. A real bestseller, Dr. Johnson!

I realize I've painted quite a grim picture, but isn't that the picture of reality for many of you right now? Can we take a moment to just hold space for how much it sucks?

Maybe you're the kind of person that has lived in the "it sucks" thoughts daily for the past two years, and you're quite accustomed to it. Maybe you're someone who likes to look for the positive in everything and perhaps that doesn't allow you to really look critically at your own reality. If you're one of the latter, I invite you to sit with the "suck" for a couple of minutes and allow yourself to lament the parts of yourself you've given tirelessly for the past few years.

If you're the former, you'll be happy to know that this whole book isn't a lament of what has been. It's primarily a look at what could be.

You've probably already noticed that the chapters are short and the book itself is brief. Each section and each chapter stand alone. That is deliberate. When you're overwhelmed and burned out, who has time or motivation to read a lengthy, complicated book about burnout??

I hope the format of this book helps you to read a little bit at a time so you can make sustainable changes and celebrate every little step in the direction of joy, energy, and connection.

You weren't meant to live a life of burnout with a hint of joy; you were meant to live a life drenched in joy, with some come-and-go feelings of burnout.

Let's work together to get you there, one short chapter at a time.

- Jen Johnson, PhD

Part One

VOW TO HONOR OUR HUMANNESS

"I am just a human being trying to make it in a world that is rapidly losing its understanding of being human."

— JOHN TRUDELL

WHAT IS HUMANNESS?

I have to be honest that when I first developed this part of my burnout prevention and recovery model, I knew that the word "humanness" encapsulated the essence of what I was trying to capture, but I didn't even know if it was a real word. It is, as it turns out, and it simply means "the quality of being human."

When I think about the quality of being human, I think about the fact that I'm a biological being with physiological limitations, not an immortal robot with endless energy. I require food, water, shelter, and rest for survival. I think about my vulnerability, evidenced by the fact that I make mistakes because I'm not perfect. I think about my need to intentionally connect with other human beings and be accepted and loved by them, despite knowing they could reject me. I think about the fragility of my body and the sensitivity of my soul.

In a world that values productivity and is always demanding more, I often wonder where we fit in as humans - as human educators. As we embark on the first part of our journey together, I want you to consider in what ways you've lost sight of your humanness.

- What superhuman expectations have subconsciously become normal?
- Are you aware of the role being human plays in the experience of burnout?
- Are there healthy changes you would make if you could see your humanness more clearly?

Chapter One

THE ELEPHANT IN THE ROOM

*E*very time I pick up a "self-help" book, I feel a little skeptical. I wonder: *Does this person really get me? Does this Dr. Whoever have some magical answer that I haven't run across yet? Is this just gonna be another book telling me a whole list of things I need to do that I'm not doing?*

I want to help you understand where I come from and why I'm invested in teacher health, because without my "why," this is, in many ways, just another book, and I am just another Dr. Whoever.

I began teaching in K-12 schools back in 2009 in a rural area. For a year and a half, I was the only Deaf Education teacher in my school, then I did some itinerant teaching for a few months. If you're not familiar with itinerant teaching, it's when you pack your whole class-room into a car and travel around the countryside to different rural schools serving one kid here and two kids there. It's a unique teaching experience for sure.

I changed districts between my second and third year teaching, and taught in a large, urban district in North Texas until I became an Instructional Specialist in Special Education. When working full-time and doing doctoral studies full-time started to make me feel like I couldn't be a human with realistic limits, I left K-12 and started super-vising student teachers and interns nationwide, along with teaching college courses, which I still do on an adjunct-basis because I'm invested in the future of K-12 schools.

My first personal encounter with burnout happened in my third year of teaching, when I had a particularly challenging student in my class. For a variety of reasons, it took quite a long time for me to get support, and by the time I did, I was crispy. Burned to an absolute crisp.

Like many of you, I didn't have the life circumstances that allowed me to leave the profession, nor did I really want to leave. So I stayed, and frankly, I suffered as I tried to figure out how to help myself. After doing my own research into evidence-based practices for burnout recovery and seeing a Licensed Professional Counselor to help me implement them, I figured out some strategies that worked well enough for me to stay in the classroom, but I remember thinking there had to be a better way - a way to do my job well and feel better than just "okay."

My second up-close encounter with burnout was when I worked as an Instructional Specialist in Special Education. I supported a campus that had a unit that served children with challenging behavior. The entire year I worked with the unit, it was a revolving door of different teachers, teaching assistants, and substitutes. All of them communicated similar thoughts and emotions to mine as I tried, and failed, to support them enough for them to stay. The resounding theme was: "I'm exhausted. I'm struggling to care. I don't have it in me to implement any of these behavior management plans with fidelity."

I now recognize all of those individuals were experiencing burnout. They didn't need me to help them with student strategies. They needed me to bring a toolkit of strategies to help them learn how to thrive in a difficult environment as human beings with needs and emotions.

When I went back to school to study emotional and behavioral disorders, I became interested in what needed to change to be able to retain teachers who work with students with emotional and behavioral disorders. My work related to teacher burnout, including this book, are an outflow of the study that started then and continues into the present.

I know you'd rather poke your eyeball out with a freshly sharpened Ticonderoga pencil than have one more person tell you that you are burned out because you aren't doing "self-care" correctly.

WHAT IS THE ELEPHANT IN THE ROOM?

Self-care.

The elephant in the room of this book is self-care. I can't read your mind, but if I could I bet on some level you're wondering, "Is this another book that is going to tell me to just 'go do self-care'?"

I know the word "self-care" has been thrown around like a magical solution since the pandemic started, and you're tired of hearing it. I know you'd rather poke your eyeball out with a freshly sharpened Ticonderoga pencil than have one more person tell you that you are burned out because you aren't doing "self-care" correctly.

Self-care is a ginormous elephant. It's so big you can't see around it, and it's more distracting than the smell of a 6th grade classroom full of kids after recess who haven't started wearing deodorant. Everything about shaming people into "self-care" is intrusive and undesirable.

Our culture has made self-care into something based in capitalism. It's bath bombs and manicures and massages and take-out and vacations. And if you can't afford those things, you need to work harder and make more money so you can take care of yourself! Is that the message you get? I sure do! The ads online. The TV commercials. All pointing to this life of luxury that is beyond my financial means and takes up more time than I seem to have available. It requires more than I have to give and requires resources I cannot fathom, which causes me to feel shame. It makes me feel less-than-human.

This book is NOT about capitalistic self-care. In fact, I know the word "self-care" is emotionally triggering for a lot of teachers after the way it has been misused during the pandemic, so I've done my best to avoid using it in this book, except in specific instances.

Instead, this book is about real, evidence-based, practical strategies that you can weave into your life that will help you activate calm, relaxation, and pleasure in the middle of your chaotic, stressful, and time-finite day.

I'm kicking the elephant out of the room. Big, distracting, smelly ideas that make you feel 100% responsible for burnout are not allowed here.

And now that we have that out of the way, let's move forward with the hope and expectation that answers do exist, and some of them may be found in these pages. Let's move forward honoring the fact that we are humans with limited resources and need strategies that work within our limitations.

Action:
Think About - Write About - Talk About

- What excites you about reading this book?
- What gives you that yucky knot in your stomach?
- What could this book say that would feel like a flood of relief?
- What could this book say that would make you pitch it in the trash?

Chapter Two

BURNOUT IN A NUTSHELL

*W*hen I think back on the time in my career when I experienced the highest level of burnout, I remember feeling a lot of different emotions. I felt sad because how I was experiencing teaching was not what I had dreamed about when I decided to become one.

I felt guilty because by the end of the year I was treading water, and I thought my students weren't getting the kind of education they deserved. I had started the year as an excellent teacher, but as the burnout got worse and worse, I knew my teaching was not as effective as I wanted it to be.

I felt shame because, for the life of me, I couldn't figure out what was wrong with me and how to fix myself.

I felt angry that I wasn't getting the help and support I needed for a student with severe behavioral challenges, and that caused me to feel resentful and cynical not only about my leadership, but the educational system as a whole.

But most of all, I felt tired. And it wasn't the kind of tired that a week off or a nap was going to remedy. It was the kind of tired that reaches down into the depths of your soul to suck out every last bit of joy and hope. I was soul-tired.

I didn't even have a word for it, really. I didn't recognize it as "burnout" in a scientific sense. I just knew I felt miserable and hopeless about my job.

When I first stumbled upon the burnout literature years later, I remember feeling seen and known. I didn't know these scientists whose work I was reading, but I had this deep sense of being understood and affirmed.

Knowledge doesn't cure burnout, but my hope is that understanding the science behind your burnout might help you feel compassion for yourself and remind you that what is happening to you is a real, scientific, measurable phenomenon. You aren't weak-willed, lazy, or defective. You are experiencing something very real that has been studied for over 50 years.

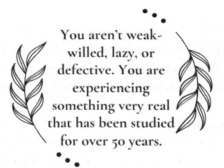

You aren't weak-willed, lazy, or defective. You are experiencing something very real that has been studied for over 50 years.

Dr. Christina Maslach, a social psychologist, started studying occupational burnout in the 1970s, and her work eventually led to the operational definition, predictors, and measurement of burnout that we still use today. Her research showed that there were three primary dimensions of burnout: exhaustion, depersonalization, and reduced professional efficacy (Maslach & Leiter, 2017). Let's look at each of these dimensions individually and unpack the practical reality of each.

EXHAUSTION

The most obvious and commonly reported symptom associated with burnout is emotional and physical exhaustion.

Exhaustion is not simply "tired." Exhaustion is a deep level of soul-draining fatigue that lingers no matter how much sleep you get, but finding rhythms of true rest are crucial.

Exhaustion alone doesn't constitute burnout though, so simply addressing exhaustion doesn't cure it. This is one of the most tricky and deceiving things about burnout. I remember thinking that summer break or winter break or a day off was going to make me feel better. I thought I would feel rested, rejuvenated, and ready to tackle all the challenges of teaching again. But it never worked that way. That's because simply taking time off, even long amounts of time, does not cure burnout. If you go into the same environment with the same coping strategies, burnout will return as quickly as the relief came.

DEPERSONALIZATION

Perhaps the hardest aspect of burnout to understand is depersonalization because it's not a word we use a lot in our daily lives. It looks a lot like cynicism, but with nuance.

When we experience depersonalization at work, it means we emotionally and cognitively distance ourselves from the work and the relationships that exist in that space. We build up a wall to protect ourselves from the overwhelm, and we stop seeing what makes our students and colleagues unique, making it easier to disconnect from their humanity. The more we disconnect from their humanity, the more we experience a change in our relationship with them.

REDUCED PROFESSIONAL EFFICACY

Finally, we see a drop in our effectiveness as teachers. We feel ineffective, and in many cases we actually *are* less effective.

I don't want you to internalize this as shameful because there are real, legitimate reasons why this occurs. If you are exhausted and disconnected, it is practically impossible to maintain the level of preparation and execution it takes to be effective in the 21st century, almost-post-pandemic classroom. You literally don't have it in you, and that is okay. That is why we are here together in this space, looking for a gentle way forward - a human way forward.

Do you recognize yourself in this chapter? Do you feel the exhaustion and disconnection? Do you know deep down your effectiveness has wavered?

If you do, I'm so glad you picked up this book. You may feel like you are lying in the middle of a burned-up field of grass, discouraged and without hope, but I assure you, dear friend, that under the surface there is movement already. Under the surface of the soil of your soul is a tiny little seed, and this book is the water and the nutrition that your tiny soul seed needs to break out of its shell. It's going to take time, and it's going to take patience, and it's going to take trust in the process. But if you'll stick with me, I am certain the hard shell will break open and bring forth new life.

Action:
Just how burned out are you?

If you're curious about your level of burnout you can go to www.mindgarden.com and select the Maslach Burnout Toolkit for Educators. It's $25 for the administration of the test and the report. You can also go to www.teachercarenetwork.com/book for a direct link.

Chapter Three

THRIVING

When I was in college, I adopted an injured fish. A girl down the hall bought two, and one of them was determined to kill the other, so they had to be separated. I eagerly volunteered to take the injured one, but that fish was never right after we separated him from the other. He just kind of floated at the top of the tank like he was dead, though he was still alive. When I'd put food in the tank, he'd muster up all the energy he had and dart down to the food. As soon as it hit his mouth, he would relax and float back to the top. I learned later he had an injured swim bladder, but I was 18 and clueless at the time.

The whole experience reminds me of burnout.

I know many of you feel like you were in a fight for the past two years. You were fighting for the food to feed your soul, with an underlying condition of burnout to boot, and you just didn't know what to do. You got beat up by the other fish in the tank and eventually you just floated. And floated and floated. And then you realized, Gahhhhh I have to feed myself or I'm never going to get better! And everyone yelled, "YEAH, FEED YOURSELF!" So you darted down and grabbed a quick bite for relief and then you floated again. And floated and floated and floated. Some fish jumped right out of that tank onto the dorm room floor because they didn't want to do it anymore, but you stayed there: floating, floating, floating.

To be clear, in this silly analogy, these are the players:

The fish tank is your work environment, in which you've been fighting some gnarly fish, like a pandemic, virtual and hybrid learning, new policies, mask wearing all day long, keeping children 6 feet apart, risking your health to show up at work, filling the learning gaps, new legislation, racial injustice, and on and on.

Those quick bites of food you darted down for were one complimentary yoga session, changing grade levels, changing schools, getting a massage, taking a hot bath, taking a day off, or getting a pedicure. They gave some relief, but the burnout just came back, and as a result, you were just floating. You felt hopeless, discouraged, and tired, and that meant you did the minimum to survive.

Some teachers didn't make it. They jumped out of the tank into corporate America, insurance sales, edTech, private tutoring, and other careers, but you stayed.

I don't want you to keep floating and diving until you decide to jump out of the tank onto the dorm room floor of another career. I want you to THRIV™ your way back to calm, contented joy!

WHAT DOES IT MEAN TO THRIV™?

In this book, we will work our way through a model for burnout prevention and recovery called THRIV™.

THRIV™ stands for:
  Tend to Yourself
  Harness Social Support
  Recharge Through Detachment
  Ignite Compassion Satisfaction
  Vow to Honor Your Humanness

Instead of starting at the top, we're starting at the bottom. You already know this strategy because it's how we teach kids new concepts. We look at each standard, and design an assessment. Then we conduct a task analysis, or look at a curriculum document, to figure out what all the prerequisite skills are that a student needs to be able to master the standard we are targeting. We give a diagnostic assessment, figure out where we need to start, and off we go strategically working our way to the standard.

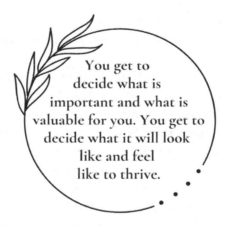

You get to decide what is important and what is valuable for you. You get to decide what it will look like and feel like to thrive.

We will start with **Vowing to Honor Our Humanness**. I think of it like print awareness in the process of teaching literacy. Once we can orient ourselves in the context of our lives, we're ready for the nitty gritty of strategy, but first, we need to realize the limitations and boundaries that come along with being human.

Next, we'll figure out how to **Ignite Compassion Satisfaction** because one of the quickest ways to the exit ramp in education is to not have any evidence of your effectiveness and success as a teacher.

Once we've established routines for building compassion satisfaction, we'll learn strategies for **Recharging Through Detachment** because wearing the educator hat 24/7 is not healthy nor reasonable for emotional health.

After that, we'll dive into how to **Harness Social Support** to get the most out of your relationships with family, fellow-educators, non-educator friends, and support networks.

Then we'll end with an organizational strategy, **Tending to Your-self**, where we'll bring all the pieces together into a plan.

DEFINING YOUR VERSION OF THRIVING

Before we jump into the content of the book and talk about strategies for recovery and sustainability, we have to decide what the standard will be.

The nice part about this "standard" is that *you* get to decide what it is and what it isn't. You get to decide what is important and what is valuable for you. You get to decide what it will look like and feel like to thrive.

When I think of thriving, I think about words like comfort, ease, calm, and pleasure. I think about health and compassion and care and love. I think about enjoying my life as a human being instead of trudging through it like a robot whose battery is almost depleted.

I think about waking up in the morning, leisurely drinking a cup of coffee, showering, dressing, and driving in the slow lane to work while I listen to songs that fill my soul with hope. I think about how I feel in my body - calm, nourished, and light. And I think about what I'll do if my body becomes activated, needy, and heavy. I think about having a posture of self-compassion towards myself and the peace that will flow from that.

But that's me.

What does it mean for you to feel like you're thriving?

Action:
Think About - Write About - Talk About

• What does a "day in the life" of thriving look like?
• What outcome are you seeking?
• How will it feel? How will you know if you're experiencing a thriving life?

Chapter Four

HUMANS HAVE NEEDS

As educators, most of us are familiar with Maslow's Hierarchy of Needs. It's in almost every introductory psychology textbook and often discussed in the context of services offered to students, like free breakfast and lunch, and why students with certain life circumstances struggle to learn.

Interestingly, there's very little empirical research on the hierarchical nature of this theory because it's logically "debunkable" without study. There are many examples of people placing belonging or safety above physiological needs (e.g. diet culture places belonging over physiological needs; sacrificing personal safety for a child places safety over physiological needs). As a result, I'd like to reframe how we were taught to think about needs. I'd like us to move away from "requirements to exist" to "what I need to thrive."

If I asked you if your needs were getting met based on Maslow's Hierarchy of Needs, most of you would say "yes." You have access to food, water, and shelter. You feel relatively safe in your environment and you feel like there's at least one place you belong, whether that's through involvement in an organization or through a relationship with a person. Maybe you don't feel "self-actualized," but we're all works in progress, right?

Needs are so much deeper than the bare minimum needed to survive. Many of you picked up this book because you feel like you've been in "survival mode" as a teacher for several years, and you NEED something to change. That need is a real, legitimate, psychological need. You might not die from not having your psychological needs met, like you would die from not having access to food or water, but it doesn't make the needs any less legitimate.

There's extensive research that tells us there are three psychological needs that must be met to thrive: competence, relatedness, and autonomy (Deci & Ryan, 2000; Pittman & Zeigler, 2007). These needs must be met in our personal and professional lives for us to experience a sense of well-being and thriving. So what do these needs mean?

Once I realize I have a need, I have power.

Competence is being able to change the things you want to change in your personal and professional life.

Relatedness is how close you feel to others in your personal and professional life. Autonomy is the perception that you're choosing and in control of the activities in your personal and professional life.

Sometimes, when we are experiencing something uncomfortable emotionally and we're unable to identify the cause, it's helpful to ask, "What need do I have that isn't being met in this moment?"

I often start with physiological needs and ask, "Am I hungry? Am I thirsty? Am I tired? Do I feel safe in my body?" If the answer to all those is "yes," then I ask, "Am I feeling incompetent, like I can't do something I want to do or make a change I want to make?" "Am I feeling isolated or lonely, or in need of connection?" "Am I feeling out of control of my life, like other people or circumstances are exerting control over me and my will?" Often the answer to one of those questions is "yes." I have a psychological need that is not being met.

Once I realize I have a need, I have power. I can practice radical acceptance that I am a human being with human needs that sometimes are not met, and that leads me to be able to grieve that particular need not being met, or it gives me the energy to seek out support for that need.

When you can recognize a pattern of need and you don't know how to get that need met, it's helpful to talk to a family member, friend, coach, or mental health counselor to come up with a strategy. Often we are too close to our own situations and experiences to see simple solutions that others can recognize with ease.

Action:
Think About - Write About - Talk About

Do a quick mental appraisal of your personal and professional life.
• In what ways do you feel competent or incompetent?
• Where do you experience strong connection, and where is relatedness lacking?
• In what areas of your life do you experience autonomy, and where do you long for more?

Chapter Five

HUMANS EXPERIENCE STRESS IN THEIR BODIES

We live an embodied existence - meaning that, without our bodies, we cease to exist. I know that seems like a "duh" statement, but sometimes I think we forget the significance of our bodies. Sometimes we value our thoughts and intellect, our impact and contributions, over the very bodies that give us the ability to think, reason, and make a difference in the world.

I think we also forget that while our society has developed at unprecedented rates in the past century or so, our brains have not evolved as quickly.

Our brains are activated in physiological ways by stressors. Primitively, these stressors were lions, tigers, and bears. *Oh, my!* Today, our stressors are car rider pickup duty, last minute IEP meetings, paperwork deadlines, data collection, upset parents, state testing, pandemics, learning gaps, and the cafeteria being out of your favorite ice cream. I joke, but if you are like me when I was a teacher, and treat yourself to a cone every Friday, you know the unexplainable stress when the lunch lady lets you down!

Because stress is a physiological response, not a cognitive response, simply "finishing" the stressful situation or event isn't adequate to alleviate the physiological stress response. We may feel emotional relief sometimes, but our bodies are still full of stress hormones.

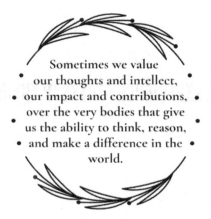

Sometimes we value our thoughts and intellect, our impact and contributions, over the very bodies that give us the ability to think, reason, and make a difference in the world.

In their book *Burnout: The Secret to Closing the Stress Response Cycle*, the Nagoski sisters describe 7 evidence-based ways to inform our bodies that we have defeated the lion and completed the stress cycle. They include: physical activity, breathing, positive social interaction, laughter, affection, crying, and creative expression.

By engaging in these activities regularly, our brain processes the hormones and receives the message that the danger has passed. When we don't regularly help our body clear itself of stress hormones, we live in a state of chronic stress, which has far-reaching health impacts on our physical health, and puts us at greater risk for burnout and depression (Bakusik et al., 2017).

By honoring our body's need to physiologically process stress, our brains are able to shift from the limbic system (where stress lives) into the prefrontal cortex that gives us the thinking and reasoning skills that help us impact the world in the ways we desire.

Action:
Give Your Brain a Break

Pick a few of the evidence-based ways of closing the stress response cycle and "try them on" today.

Chapter Six

HUMANS GET SICK

I started my very first day as a brand new teacher living in a borrowed trailer on an RV camping site because I didn't have a place to live yet. On the 3rd day of new teacher training, I locked myself out of the trailer in my pajamas with my dog. After an hour of trying to figure out how to pick the lock, I realized I could maybe crawl through the dirty clothes chute that went from the underside storage of the trailer into the cabinet in the bathroom to get back into the trailer. And then I got stuck in the laundry chute, half inside the bathroom cabinet and half underneath the trailer. I started laughing hysterically, and subsequently crying, but eventually shimmied my way up into the cabinet, crawled out of the cabinet, threw on my clothes, and raced to work.

Needless to say, my principal was not impressed, but I felt like I proved myself that year. My evaluation was "Exceeds Expectations" across the board, and included a note that she had never given "Exceeds" to a new teacher before. I was pretty proud of myself, and I still have the note she wrote me after my observation tucked away in a journal.

The next year in August I had to have a reproductive procedure the week of teacher in-service. That weekend my husband went to spend the weekend with his parents, and when he got home that Sunday night before the first day of school, he told me he wanted a divorce.

I was blindsided and devastated, but I showed up to teach on the first day of school with a smile plastered across my face and a fake pep in my step. At the end of the day, I asked for a couple of days off to find a place to live, and frankly, to just take a moment to be a human being. Unfortunately, my principal was not supportive. She reminded me that I had missed the entire week of in-service and suggested that I was letting my team down by taking time off because no one could use sign language to communicate with my students except me. I nodded and agreed to continue working, went back to my classroom, and collapsed onto the floor, sobbing.

I was not okay, but I really lacked the skills to advocate further, and my principal lacked skills, too. She was, no doubt, feeling the pressure of maintaining the status of Distinguished Elementary School, and my students were significantly behind their peers academically. There was literally no one else on campus who could even communicate with my students, much less teach them.

With the help of an incredible co-worker, I found an apartment near the school and signed a lease for $425 a month - you can imagine how fancy and adequate it was based on the price.

I continued to have reproductive-related emergencies, often going to the emergency room at night and showing up to teach the next morning. These issues had been escalating for years and treatment options finally ran out on a Wednesday in October. I found out I needed a hysterectomy imminently, and out of fear of further disappointing my principal, I asked if I could take a risk and wait a couple of days to make sure my class was covered and lesson plans were made. The doctor reluctantly agreed.

I informed my principal as soon as I got home that I would be out for 6-8 weeks for the procedure and she emailed me in the middle of the night to tell me to come by her office the next day after school. I assumed it was because there was some paperwork she needed me to fill out.

When I showed up in her office on the last day of work before a medically-necessary, life-changing procedure, she told me that I wasn't a team player, that I had never been a team player, and that she had known since I missed that 3rd morning of teacher training because I allegedly "locked myself out of my trailer" that I wasn't a team player. She told me I was selfish for having the procedure in the middle of the year when I was the only teacher on campus certified to teach my students, and that if I didn't plan on changing my ways, to not come back after my medical leave.

> You deserve compassion and empathy and love and kindness, and even if that won't come from outside yourself, I want you to find that compassion, love, and kindness within yourself.

The condemnation for being a human with human needs sank deep into my soul that day.

After returning to the classroom, the harassment continued until I was traumatized, severely depressed, and in need of significant psychological intervention. The failure of my body to be "good enough" to conceive, my husband leaving me, the reality that I would never birth a baby, and the hostile work environment was more than my human body, mind, and soul could handle. I was admitted to a partial hospitalization program for 5 weeks to help me recover from the trauma.

I returned to the district after my hospitalization ended, was reassigned to a new job, and my new boss was briefed about why I was moved. I can only assume that she was frustrated with the situation because from my first day back, she made it clear I was not wanted.

I resigned, without board approval, in March of that year, at the recommendation of my psychiatrist and mental health counselor. I knew it was possible that I would never be hired again because I was leaving mid-year, but I didn't have a choice. It was the job or my mental health.

I almost quit teaching permanently after that. I moved home for the summer and got a job at the local university working in PR, but the passion in me to work with deaf and hard-of-hearing kids couldn't be squelched. As soon as I started seeing job postings for deaf education teachers, I couldn't deny who I was at my core: a teacher.

I applied in a large, urban district, interviewed the next week, and was completely honest about what had happened in my previous district. One of the women who interviewed me became one of my long-term mentors. A few years later she told me the minute I walked out the door, she called her boss and said, "I can't believe they ran this teacher off. Hire her today!" I remember crying on the way home the day she told me, because I was still working on believing that I was a good teacher after having been treated so terribly in my former district. I worked in that same school and district for the rest of my time in public education, and I still consider it home. *Go Miller Mavs!* I eventually found the love of my life, who accepts me in all of my humanness and imperfection, and three years ago we adopted a little boy. *Yay for a joyous turn of events!*

Maybe you don't have a story like mine, but I am willing to bet that you can relate in some way to being mistreated, shamed, or doubted because you needed to take a sick day or 10 sick days. Maybe the toxic expectation came from your boss or maybe the toxic expectation came from within yourself. Regardless of where the pressure comes from to show up when you should stay home, know you aren't alone.

In the Teacher Care Network Support Community, a community I facilitate on Facebook, I've approved multiple posts just this school year that follow the same pattern: "I am sick and need to stay home, but if I do, XYZ will happen. What should I do?"

The resounding feedback is always, "TAKE THE DAY!"

It's hard, and it's scary, and sometimes you will get treated less than human when you do so (by those in the system, or by your own self!), but hear me when I say that you, my dear friend, are a complex, beautiful human being who deserves to rest when you are sick. You deserve compassion and empathy and love and kindness, and even if that won't come from outside yourself, I want you to find that compassion, love, and kindness within yourself.

If you can't find it *yet,* please come into the Teacher Care Network Support Community and let us show you compassion, love, and kindness there. You are a beautiful, intricate, physiological and psychological masterpiece. Take that reality and plant it deep down in your soul. Breathe in the self-compassion, and take the sick day. Here are a few strategies to help you make the healthy choice.

HAVE A COMMUNICATION PLAN

Create an email saved in your email drafts to send on days you are sick. If you are required to send texts or make phone calls, draft a text or phone script in the Notes section of your phone. That will get you past the paralysis of not knowing what to say in the moment.

HAVE A PLAN FOR SUB PLANS

Figure out a sub-plan strategy that works for you and your team. Maybe that means every teacher on your team makes 2 days of sub plans. If you have 5 teachers on your team and you all share, you now have 10 days of sub plans. Dedicate time over the next few weeks to make the copies and put everything into a sub crate. Make it work for you, and if you need ideas or help troubleshooting, hop into the Teacher Care Network Support Community (www.teachercarenetwork.com/community) and ask!

Action:
Think About - Write About - Talk About

• Reflect on your beliefs about taking sick days.
• Identify anything getting in the way of taking care of your body.
• Formulate a plan to help you make a human choice next time you're sick.

Part Two

IGNITE COMPASSION SATISFACTION

"This is a moment of suffering. Suffering is part of life. May I be kind to myself in this moment. May I give myself the compassion I need."

— DR. KRISTIN NEFF

Whenever I want to see a teacher's eyes light up, I ask them about the notes, arts, and gifts they've received from students over the years. The appreciation and love conveyed by students and parents throughout a teacher's career are the crowning moments. They are the moments when you say to yourself, "This is why I do this job."

The past few years have been difficult, and suffering has abounded throughout our society. Whether we experienced it personally, or watched others endure it, we have all been impacted by suffering.

Sometimes the suffering we watch students experience or listen to them describe can have profound impacts on our well-being. Being an observer of tragedy and experiencing the impacts of caring can lead us to question why we do the work we do, and lead us to experience profoundly deep emotions.

In this part of the book, we'll look at how burnout contributes to compassion fatigue, and learn about a way to combat it: building compassion satisfaction. Compassion satisfaction is a measure of the positive feelings and experiences someone has when they think about their job as a teacher, and it helps fight against the feelings of fatigue that arise from caring for students who have experienced difficult life circumstances and trauma.

Chapter Seven

COMPASSION FATIGUE

"I've cared too well, for too long, with too little support, and I just can't care anymore."

I've heard this sentiment echo throughout hundreds of conversations with teachers in the past few years. You have poured your whole heart and soul into helping the students you teach. You've worked countless hours of overtime. You've completed your "other duties as assigned" with a smile on your face. You've stayed up late crafting incredible lessons with impeccable, evidence-based strategies. You've responded to every parent concern within 24 hours. You've listened to your students' heartbreaking stories of homelessness and food insecurity and domestic violence, and you've imagined late at night what it's like for them when they aren't at school. You've learned of school shooting after school shooting, and you've imagined over and over and over what you would do to protect the children in your care.

Then a thought arises that you just can't shake, "I just can't do this anymore. I can't care anymore. It's killing me to care."

I want to help you understand where that thought and feeling comes from, because I think it will give you hope to learn that what you're experiencing has a name and is a studied phenomenon.

As someone who spends the majority of my time listening to teachers talk about their burnout, I noticed early on that teachers talked frequently about the impact of listening to their students recount traumatic experiences, and the impact of school violence on their mental health. Like any educational psychologist would, I dug into the literature to explore the connection between burnout and what I recognized as secondary traumatic stress. What I found was research about compassion fatigue, another term often used interchangeably with secondary traumatic stress, and while it isn't talked about much in the education space, it is heavily studied in other helping professions, like nursing, social work, and counseling.

Compassion fatigue is measured by determining levels of burnout, secondary traumatic stress and compassion satisfaction (Stamm, 2010).

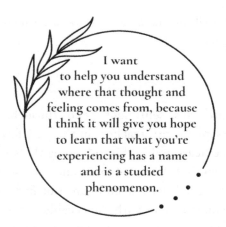

I want to help you understand where that thought and feeling comes from, because I think it will give you hope to learn that what you're experiencing has a name and is a studied phenomenon.

In chapter 2, we defined burnout as a combination of exhaustion, depersonalization, and lack of professional efficacy (Maslach & Leiter, 2017). Secondary traumatic stress is the emotional distress you experience in response to hearing the traumatic experiences of others (McCann & Pearlman, 1990; Sprang et al., 2019). This could include directly hearing about it from a victim or being immersed in media that provide video, photographs, and descriptions that function as direct accounts. For example, you could hear a colleague who was involved in a school shooting describe it or you could immerse yourself in enough media that it's as if you heard a direct account.

Recently, a high school teacher with whom I attend yoga class shared that she had been having nightmares and anxiety about school shootings. This was shortly after a high school two hours away had a school shooting. It didn't happen to her, but she heard about it enough and had imagined how she would handle it enough that it impacted her functioning. Stories like this are not uncommon in my workshops, in one-on-one coaching, and in the online Teacher Care Network Support Community. Teachers are experiencing burnout, but they're also experiencing trauma.

I think it's important to talk about the existence of secondary traumatic stress because sometimes we think we're experiencing burnout when what we're really experiencing is a combination of burnout and secondary traumatic stress, and trauma requires professional help.

In terms of prevention, increasing compassion satisfaction, or the positive feelings and experiences we have about being caring educators, helps us build resilience to fight both burnout and secondary traumatic stress. Though this book is primarily targeting burnout prevention and recovery strategies, many of the strategies throughout the book are also effective in building compassion fatigue resilience, so if you implement strategies from all of the parts of the book, you are building protection against burnout and compassion fatigue.

Action:
Seek Help, Offer Help

If you think you are experiencing secondary traumatic stress, please seek help from a mental health professional. You can find professionals in your area by going to www.psychologytoday.com.

If you're a teacher leader, consider becoming trained and certified in Mental Health First Aid so you know how to recognize the signs of a mental health crisis, engage in difficult conversations, and connect colleagues to professional providers.

Chapter Eight

JOURNALING: THE CONTENT

Compassion Satisfaction Journaling

*I*magine you're in the jungle. You're living in the time of cavemen, and you're out hunting for your dinner. You hear beautiful birds singing, followed by a big, terrifying lion roar. I wonder if you'd pay attention to the beautiful birds or figure out the location and situation with the lion?

I think most of us, without hesitation, would say we'd attune to the lion, because we all have an innate desire to survive. Once I've managed the lion situation, I might stop and enjoy the birds, but my primary focus is on staying away from those sharp teeth and getting out of that area alive.

Now imagine a few weeks pass and I come back to that same location. Because I encountered that lion last time I was in the area, I'm probably going to be thinking, *Is that lion still around here?*, not *Are those beautiful birds still here?* This is because our brains are designed to attune to the negative first to keep us safe (Veerapa et al., 2020).

So let's translate this situation to the 21st century school where we are providing interventions for significant behavioral issues, dealing with harmful TikTok challenges, and trying to figure out if this is actually an active shooter this time, or just a prank. Pile on top of that the conflict I'm having with my co-teacher and the jammed copier and the dang goodie table on the week I'm really trying to be more balanced with my eating. I bet you could make me a mile long list of everything that's going wrong at your school and in your district.

It's a lot easier to remember the things that go wrong than the things that go right, isn't it?

> When we have the little voice in our head that tells us we're no good at being a teacher, we need evidence to prove to us that we actually are, indeed, good teachers who are good at teaching and caring.

In order to combat against the tendency our brains have to focus on what goes wrong, we need a powerful tool to help us remember things that go right. When we have the little voice in our head that tells us we're no good at being a teacher, we need evidence to prove to us that we actually are, indeed, good teachers who are good at teaching and caring.

The good, positive feelings we have about how effective we are at caring for other people is called compassion satisfaction. It's particularly important in professions, like teaching, where we are at risk of developing compassion fatigue, which we discussed in the previous chapter.

THE CONTENT OF A COMPASSION FATIGUE JOURNAL

One of the most effective strategies I've found for teachers is to keep some kind of compassion satisfaction "journal." I put "journal" in quotes because we all have different strengths and different preferences when it comes to creating a space for remembering our wins.

The purpose of the "journal" is to have a place where you can go on the days you are feeling deflated to remember the good you have done as a teacher. Here are some things you could include:

- pictures
- quotes from students, parents, co-workers, or supervisors
- anecdotal stories of student progress in academic areas
- anecdotal stories of student progress in social and emotional areas
- anecdotal stories about making a difference in your students' lives
- funny stories that remind you why you love working with students
- funny stories that remind you why you love working with other teachers
- copies of emails and notes from parents and supervisors
- notes and artwork you've received from students
- a weekly note about one thing that happened that week that makes you want to return to school next week

Along with each piece of evidence, you'll make a quick note about how it felt when you received that feedback, observed that growth, or experienced that success. The content might look something like this:

Judy requested help for the first time today.	I felt so proud. We have tried so many strategies, and I'm so happy we found something that works for her.
The principal complimented my classroom management today.	I felt so relieved because sometimes I think she doesn't see how hard I'm working with the kids. I'm so glad she sees the efforts I'm making.
Everyone passed the test this week.	I am so excited because I tried a new strategy to teach the content and it worked!

Action:
Track Your Wins

Jot down a few wins you've experienced this week and how it made you feel. In the next chapter, we'll consider different ways of keeping track of our wins.

Chapter Nine

JOURNALING: THE PROCESS
Compassion Satisfaction Journaling

*N*ow that you know what to include in your compassion satisfaction journal, let's explore popular options of keeping records that align with your strengths. I'm going to give you a few categories that most people fall within and some examples, but the possibilities are endless. The most important part of compassion satisfaction "journaling" isn't the avenue that you use to record your feelings and experience. It's the act of doing it and looking back on it again and again and again.

THE TRADITIONAL JOURNALIST

The Traditional Journalist already keeps a written journal, or wants to start! If the idea of getting a new paper journal is exciting and motivating, this might be a good option for you. If you already journal on a regular basis, I recommend getting a separate journal for this task. When it's time to take a peek at the evidence that you're a good teacher, you don't want to have to dig through all the other writing to find evidence of positive feelings and experiences at work. Keep it in a separate journal or flip your journal over and start from the back so you know exactly where to go when you need it.

THE HOPEFUL-BUT-HESITANT

The Hopeful-but-Hesitant type is the teacher who is finding the concept of even having a journal overwhelming.

I recommend just starting a list. Using a notepad or the Notes app in your phone, you can write a simple phrase or sentence as a reminder of what happened and how you felt. I've included an example of what that might look like in the photo.

←   🗅 🔔 ⬇

Proof I'm a Good Teacher   ⋮

▦ ☐ Jody signed a three word utterance this week. At the beginning of the year she was using single word communication.

▦ ☐ Andrew said I'm his favorite teacher EVER.

▦ ☐ Suzie's mom emailed and said she's really been coming out of her shell since the school year started.

▦ ☐ Jose came and found me before school and said he misses me being his teacher.

▦ ☐ Students loved how I integrated the stock market into the lesson on the thousandths place.

▦ ☐ Shane asked someone at recess to play instead of sitting by himself. The social stories are working great!

THE THUMB-TYPER AND FINGER-SWIPER

The Thumb-Typer and Finger-Swiper is the teacher who would rather send an email from their phone or send a text message than open up their computer to type. There are many phone-based apps available that are excellent for keeping your journal right at your fingertips or in your hip pocket all day.

THE CREATIVE

The Creative type is the teacher who is already brainstorming what craft supplies are going to be needed to make a mixed media journal. If you want to be The Creative type, but feel intimidated, start with a notebook, some washi tape, stickers, and fun markers. Keep it messy and fun.

When I taught 1st grade in 2013, I made a scrapbook of the entire year. Of all of my years of teaching, I have the best memories of that particular year, and I think it's because I intentionally documented the good moments.

THE ECLECTIC

The Eclectic type is the teacher who either can't decide which type of journal to do, wants to do a combination of all of them, or has a super cool idea I haven't even heard of yet. You. Do. You.

Tori Smith, a teacher of the deaf in Texas, keeps reminders on a bulletin board of the positive impact she has on students' lives. You'll find post-it notes and cards full of praise and thanks and Shrinky Dink handprints of each child she has taught in the past. She also keeps student art in a file folder in the cabinet.

Action:
Just journal

Decide what kind of journal you want to make. Gather supplies and put the entries you started in the last chapter into the journal to get started. Review your journal regularly.

Part Three

RECHARGE THROUGH DETACHMENT

"These pains you feel are messengers. Listen to them."

— RUMI

Psychological detachment from work is not something that was on my radar when I was a teacher - at least I didn't have a name for it. I knew I worked a lot at home, more than people I knew who weren't teachers, and I knew I thought a lot about work, more than I perceived my friends did who worked in other professions. But I just accepted it as part of the job. All of my teacher friends did it, and it felt like an unstated expectation. We lamented it, but we didn't resist it or try to change it. We felt the pain, but we didn't listen to the pain. We just complied with the culture of our workplace without realizing we were part of the culture of our workplace.

We didn't realize the damage we were doing to ourselves by being constantly available and working well outside of the parameters of what is reasonable for a human being.

In this section, we'll take a look at what the research says about psychological detachment and practical strategies you can use to implement detachment in your professional life.

Chapter Ten

TURNING OFF WORK AND TURNING ON HOME

A few years into my teaching career, I was working in a large, urban district, and we had a tornado warning that occurred right towards the end of the day. If you aren't from a part of the world that has tornadoes, a tornado warning means a funnel cloud has been spotted near your location and you need to take cover. Elementary teacher *nightmare*, especially when you teach deaf and hard of hearing kids who you can't communicate with when they are in the proper tornado protection position on the floor.

Usually nothing happens and everyone goes on with their day. But this day was different.

On that particular day, a tornado went through an area very close to the elementary school and there was significant damage to homes, businesses, apartment complexes, and care facilities, like nursing homes.

All of my students rode the bus because I worked in a centralized program, and buses were being used to evacuate people, so we stayed super late that day until all the kids were on buses headed home. Then I headed home. As I went to turn down the road to my apartment, I was immediately visually bombarded with police cars, fire trucks, and a big Red Cross trailer.

My apartment had been hit by the tornado.

I pulled up and told the police officer I lived there, and that my dog was inside. I was hysterically crying, because my dog had been with me since college and through my hysterectomy and divorce. He directed me to an area to park, so I quickly moved my car, threw it into park, unbuckled my seatbelt, and darted towards my apartment. I was stopped by a police officer and informed that the fire department was clearing apartments and evacuating animals, and if it was safe, I might be able to grab a few things, but I needed to take a seat on the curb and wait.

I waited for about 30 minutes, and was finally reunited with my beloved Tilly and allowed to grab what I could carry from my apartment. When I walked into my bedroom, I realized that pretty much everything was destroyed. I called my co-teacher and, until my apartment was repaired, I couch-surfed. Crazy times!

When I look back on that event, and even the events surrounding my hysterectomy and divorce, I am astonished at the level to which I was able to completely compartmentalize my life. When I pulled into the school parking lot, I was able to turn my personal life off and my teaching life on. Yes, there were days I struggled, but I did it privately, with my classroom door locked, and my students never knew.

What's even more astonishing, and maybe just plain sad, is that I couldn't do the reverse at the end of the day. I couldn't turn off my teaching life, and turn on my personal life.

When I think about how to conceptualize it in education-speak, I think about the kid who has challenging behaviors at school and whose parents report no challenging behaviors at home. I think about the student whose parents report they use 4-word utterances at home to communicate and I haven't seen a 4-word utterance all year. I think about how sometimes we struggle to generalize skills to different situations and settings.

Because the stakes are high at work, I learned to turn off Jen and turn on Mrs. Johnson, but because the stakes were different, I never learned to turn off Mrs. Johnson and turn on Jen.

I have a couple of practical strategies to offer to help you make the switch.

Because the stakes are high at work, I learned to turn off Jen and turn on Mrs. Johnson, but because the stakes were different, I never learned to turn off Mrs. Johnson and turn on Jen.

THE THRESHOLD STRATEGY

The process of psychologically detaching from work can start as soon as you cross the threshold to leave your classroom.

Last year, I held a workshop about secondary traumatic stress and I invited a colleague who is a Licensed Professional Counselor to co-present with me. We took turns sharing strategies and the threshold strategy, based on the effectiveness of mindfulness (Lukin & Sammons, 2016; Sun et al, 2019; Zarate et al., 2019), is one she shared that I immediately started implementing. It has been one that requires building a bit of a mental muscle, but after consistently using it over time, it's become highly effective for me. Here are the steps to implementation:

1. Stand at the doorway and imagine all of the weight of the day stacked on your shoulders. All the deadlines. All the conflict. All the lesson planning. All the state testing. All

the stressors. Imagine that they are on your shoulders or in a backpack on your back.

2. Close your eyes and imagine lifting that heavy weight off your back and setting it down in your classroom. Visualize it sitting there on the floor, safe and sound, ready for you to pick up in the morning.

3. Walk across the threshold of the door, closing the door behind you, leaving all the stressors in the classroom.

This is not a magical strategy. It's a mindful strategy that takes time and practice to start experiencing and feeling the impacts of doing. Give it a try and see if it's good for you.

THE 50/50 COMMUTE STRATEGY

Drawing again on the research that indicates mindfulness is an effective strategy for teachers (Lukin & Sammons, 2016; Sun et al, 2019; Zarate et al., 2019), the 50/50 Commute Strategy is a mindfulness practice that was born from my own need for mindful structure in my life.

During the first couple of years of my doctoral training, I was still working in schools as a teacher and then as an instructional specialist. I attended the University of North Texas, and it was located about 55 minutes from my school. Three days a week I made that commute after work: 55 minutes to the university, and 55 minutes home.

I was balancing a lot of responsibilities at the time between work and my doctoral program. IEPs needed writing, but so did a paper on emotional behavioral disorders in children. Data needed to be collated for progress monitoring at work, but I was also running data for research. I had two very significant commitments competitively running side by side, vying for my mental attention. And that's not even considering the fact that I was a newlywed and a bonus momma to a 16-year-old boy.

I felt like my work in the district, my work at the university, and my family all deserved mental space, and transitioning between all the thoughts was overwhelming. To help me coordinate all that was happening, I started putting everything in my calendar, from the hour it took me to get ready for work in the morning to time I spent in my car commuting. Everything was on the calendar.

I'm not sure when exactly I realized this, but at some point I realized those two hours in the car everyday were a gift. I could listen to music, podcasts, and audiobooks. I could make phone calls. I could plan out entire papers in my head. And that's when the 50/50 Commute Strategy was born.

I would spend the half of the drive to the university mentally wrapping up things at work. Problem solving. Making mental checklists. Reviewing the next day in my head. And about the time that I would make the transition to a new highway, I would think to myself, "Okay. I need to get focused on grad school." I did the same thing on my way home: during that first leg of the trip, I would process all the information from class and think about next steps. When I made that highway transition I'd get excited about being half way and start thinking about home. Sometimes that meant listening to music or listening to a marriage or parenting podcast. Sometimes it meant riding in silence and thinking about how I was going to manage a conflict that had come up with my spouse or bonus son. It changed my commute, but it also transitioned my brain and put on my next "hat" really effectively.

Unless you have a commute of this length, it's probably going to look a little different for you. If you have a 15+ minute commute, you have about 7.5 minutes to allow your brain to dump work and about 7.5 minutes to fill it with home. If you have a 3 minute commute, you're probably going to need to sit in your car at school for a couple of minutes to dump before you start that short trek home. But if you have a commute that's more than a couple of minutes, here's what you'll do:

1. Determine a 50/50 landmark in your commute.
2. Purposefully and mindfully close out your day during the first half of your commute.
3. Deliberately open up your personal life on the second leg.
4. Arrive home and sit in your car for just a few seconds. Take a deep breath. Think about the comfort that awaits. And intentionally go into your home.

Action:

50/50 Your Commute

Try these strategies on your way home from work today. Journal any wins or take-aways.

Chapter Eleven

BUT I HAVE TO WORK FROM HOME!!

*E*arlier this year, I presented at the ASCD (Association for Supervision and Curriculum Development) conference and afterwards, I had the pleasure of going to dinner with a team of administrators from the North East.

When I say I had the pleasure of going with them, I mean that I was at the conference by myself, and since someone from their team was the last person to come up to me after the talk, I awkwardly blurted out, "Are you here alone or with a team?"

"With a team," he said.

"Are y'all gonna eat food tonight?" I asked casually, as if this wasn't a completely awkward question.

"Yeah. We're meeting downstairs to go to dinner."

Then in my most awkward and desperate conference moment to date, I said, "This is gonna sound weird, but can I go with you? I'm here by myself and I don't wanna eat dinner alone in my hotel room tonight."

Palm. To. Face.

Either he was genuinely excited I asked, or a really good actor - I never can tell - because 20 minutes later, I was sitting at a table in the lounge with his team chatting about my presentation.

"You know when you really had me?" he asked.

"I have absolutely no idea," I said with a smirk on my face.

"You gave all these strategies for detaching from work and then you said 'I know what you're thinking: But I have to work at home!' then BAM: a strategy for that. Read. My. Mind."

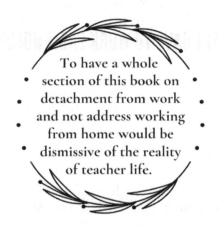

To have a whole section of this book on detachment from work and not address working from home would be dismissive of the reality of teacher life.

Remember at the beginning of the book when I said I used to be a teacher? I really was, and I really do know and understand that, as much as we don't want to work from home, sometimes it's just inevitable. Distractions, fire drills, vomiting kids and meetings during conference time. Last minute IEP modification meetings. Other duties as assigned. Complex lesson plan requirements. Work at home happens.

To have a whole section of this book on detachment from work and not address working from home would be dismissive of the reality of teacher life. As someone who has been a teacher, I know all the prioritizing and planning and rearranging in the world will not eliminate the need to work from home. My goal is not to tell you what is good or not good, but to give you a strategy to use if working from home is what is so for you.

When I talk with teachers about working from home and what that brings up for them, I often hear something that amounts to massive feelings of guilt: *I feel guilty. I feel guilty when I'm not working because I know it needs to be done, and I feel guilty when I'm working because I need to be with my family or tend to my personal life. I have to "teacher" like I don't have a family and "family" like I'm not a teacher.*

I want to help you eliminate the guilt that bubbles up from the reality of having to work from home, especially on the weekends. Here are some things to consider:

COMMUNICATE WITH PEOPLE WHO MATTER THAT YOU NEED TO WORK OVER THE WEEKEND

Who are the folks in your life who are going to be impacted by your absence? Who will need to support you whether it's through taking care of kids while you work or taking a responsibility off of your plate to create space?

SET A SPECIFIC TIME AND PLACE TO WORK

When I was a teacher, there was at least a little bit of work I had to do almost every weekend, even if it was just checking the weekly newsletter from my principal. I didn't set a time or place to do it, so it was just constantly on my mind. "Ohhh. I can't forget to get my lesson plans uploaded. Ugh. It's such a busy weekend. I don't wanna deal with it now. When am I going to get it done?"

The thoughts went on and on and on completely hijacking the time I could've spent enjoying my backyard or enjoying chatting with friends over lunch. It was always on my radar because I didn't have a plan.

When you set a time and place, your brain has the space to relax. I don't have to feel guilty for enjoying my son's soccer game because I have planned to do that IEP preparation from 3-5 pm on Sunday. And I don't have to feel guilty about working from 3-5 pm on Sunday because I've been present with my family all weekend.

AVOID MULTITASKING: IT'S A TIME-SUCK

Recently, I attended a workshop with Dr. Jane Kise on mental bandwidth, and she asked people in the audience to time how long it took to write the alphabet and numbers 1-20 in order. I decided to participate because I love a good illustration. Then she had us time ourselves again while we alternated between writing a letter and a number. I lost 60% of my efficiency multitasking between letters and numbers. I knew the science, but seeing it in action really impacted me.

To put it in context, let's imagine instead of letters and numbers we have lesson plans and Netflix.

I totally just imagined at least half of you gasping and thinking, "How did she know?!" *Smiles.* Been there. Did that. Knowing what I know now, I wish I hadn't.

Why? Because when you multitask, it takes longer to complete work.

I get why we do it. In my heart, I want to spend as much time with my son as possible, and if I work in the room with him playing or watching a cartoon, I feel better about the fact that I have to work. But the reality is that I am not present with my son. If the option is to take 2 hours of focused time away from those you love or to be in their presence without being present all day long, which would you choose? When we multitask at home, we are elongating how long work takes and ultimately spending less quality time with our families.

AVOID MULTITASKING BECAUSE IT'S A STRESSOR

Becker and colleagues (2022) published a meta-analysis earlier this year on the differences in stress system reactivity between multitasking and single-tasking. In other words, they wanted to know whether our bodies physiologically experience different amounts of stress based on whether we multitask or work on one task at a time.

What they found was that the sympathetic nervous system activity was significantly higher during multitasking and the parasympathetic nervous system activity was lower. What does this mean? It means that your brain is more stressed when you multitask than when you single-task.

When our brains become chronically stressed, we become at risk not only for physical health problems, but also for burnout and depression (Bakusik et al., 2017). I am not saying that multitasking is going to cause you to be burned out and depressed, but I am saying that it's going to contribute to your level of chronic stress, so it's wise to avoid it when possible. Is it always going to be possible? Of course not. But just being aware and mindful of the impacts of multitasking helps us make healthier decisions.

USE A FOCUS STRATEGY

If you're like me, you sit down to do some work with a cold beverage, open your computer and start working and then: ding, bing, ching, pow, drip - all the notification sounds start going off on your phone. And because your brain loves a good hit of dopamine, you glance over to see what it is. And because that hit of dopamine felt really good, you go ahead and open the email, app, text message and read it, and before you know it, you look at the time and 10 or more minutes have passed. "Ok Jen. Back on task. Back on task." Head down. Working. Two minutes later. DING. BING. CHING. POW. DRIIIIIP. I look, and another 10 minutes has passed without significant progress on the task I'm trying to get done so I can spend time with my family.

I discovered a technique during my doctoral studies that changed the way I work, called the Pomodoro Technique (Cirillo, 2006). It's simple and evidence-based, and there are many options for assistive tech to make it more enjoyable than setting a kitchen timer. When you use the Pomodoro Technique, you decide on a task you want to complete, and set a timer for 25 minutes. Once you've worked for 25 minutes, you've completed one Pomodoro. You then take a 5-minute break. You do this cycle a total of 3-4 times before taking a longer 20-30 minute break. During those breaks, I highly recommend pulling out your list of soothing emotional care interventions to help you manage your stress. If you don't have a list yet, we'll get to that in Part 5.

So that's the boring part.

Here's the fun part.

There are a number of apps that you can use for free to make the Pomodoro Technique more enjoyable. I have two favorites. On days where I just cannot for the life of me stay focused, I open an app called Forest - Focus for Productivity. In this app, I select how long I want to work, and as I work, my tree grows. If I leave the app to look at email or texts or social media, my tree dies! And y'all - for the life of me I cannot kill a virtual tree. During the pandemic, I wanted to be a plant lady and I started propagating all these plants from clippings my neighbors gave me. I gotta be honest and tell you that some of those plants died, because every time I walked by I thought, "I'll water it later." And later meant never. And they died. The actual real plants died. Give me a virtual plant though - I can't kill it. Can't. Won't. It works for me.

Another favorite is called Focus Plant. It's a gamified, more complex app. For each minute you work, you earn rain drops which you then use to water different kinds of plants until they bloom. You can build whole gardens in different locations. It's elaborate. So if keeping the plant alive doesn't keep you going, try a more gamified app like Focus Plant.

If you're not into "planty" things, you can go to your phone's app store and search "Pomodoro." There are lots of nice options.

Now onward you go with a couple of strategies for working at home!

Action:
Explore Your Options

Download a few Pomodoro Technique-based phone apps and see what works for you!

Chapter Twelve

DETACHING FROM WORK COMMUNICATIONS

*D*o you remember teaching before you could access email on your phone? What about before laptops were standard? Were you a teacher before texting was common? I was in high school when texting came into my life, but it wasn't until my third year of teaching that having 24/7 access to school-issued laptops and having email at your fingertips became an unspoken expectation.

Fast forward to today, and it's even more complex. When my son started going to daycare, there was an app we could access on our phones. It notified me every time he had a diaper change, every time he ate, and we received pictures throughout the day of him engaging in activities. As a parent, I found it really comforting, but my educator mind wondered, "How do they have time to do all this and give my child the attention he needs?!" Similar apps are now widely available to help teachers communicate with parents and they market themselves as being an easy way to keep parents informed about their child's activities and progress in the classroom.

I am not saying all this mobile technology and these ed tech products are not super cool, convenient, and helpful when used in responsible, healthy ways. As I write this, I am sitting in an AirBnB in the middle of rural Texas on a farm. I have my laptop in my lap running off battery power and I'm also listening to music through an app on my cell phone. Later, my spouse and my son will call me on a video app and I'll get to talk to them about their day face to face even though I'm 120 miles away. Technology connects us and helps us in wonderful ways.

But technology also has the potential to cause some really unfortunate, and frankly miserable, side effects and situations if we don't use our judgment to set boundaries. Researchers found that when there is an expectation from your employer to be available and responsive after contract hours, the more you use your phone, the more emotionally exhausted you become (Cheug et al., 2022). Further, Mellner (2016) found that the expectation to be available after contract hours and work-related cell phone use were associated with poor psychological detachment, and we know the ability to detach is a protective factor against development of burnout (Wendsche & Lohmann-Haislah, 2017). However, Mellner (2016) also found that when employees perceived they had boundaries in place, they were still able to successfully detach.

Changing the expectations of your school district, your principal, your co-workers, and your students' caregivers is not within your control, but setting boundaries around how you respond to those expectations is firmly in your court.

Changing the expectations of your school district, your principal, your co-workers, and your students' caregivers is not within your control, but setting boundaries around how you respond to those expectations is firmly in your court, so let's strategize around setting boundaries.

DELETE APPS AND SILENCE NOTIFICATIONS

If at all possible, delete email applications from your phone, or at least silence the notifications once you are home for the day. Communicate to supervisors, co-workers, and parents that you have a 24-hour business day turnaround time on emails, and if something needs immediate attention, a phone call is needed.

SET AN AWAY MESSAGE ON THE WEEKEND AND DURING THE SUMMER

If you are running into problems with people expecting you to respond to emails on the weekend, set an away message that communicates that you will respond to emails when you return to school on Monday.

If you aren't sure where to start, here's a template that you can adapt for your use:

> *"Thanks for emailing me. You've reached me between the end of school Friday and the beginning of school Monday. I use this time each week to recharge so I can be the best teacher possible for my students next week. I'll get back to you Monday during my designated email block. If you are a colleague and have an urgent need, please call."*

You can use the same strategy during the summer. I follow Maggie Bryant (@readingmaggie), a high school reading teacher, on Instagram, and she recently posted her away message for the summer break. It said:

> *"I am currently enjoying summer vacation with limited access to my work email. I might sporadically check and respond to emails. However, I appreciate your patience with my time offline. If your email requires a response, you can look for my reply after [insert 1st day of school here] when I return to school."*

Feel free to take these and adapt them to your voice and message.

DON'T SEND EMAILS DURING TIMES YOU WISH TO BE UNDISTURBED

If you don't want people to email you late at night or early in the morning, don't do it yourself.

Recently, I was talking with a superintendent after one of my presentations and she said, "I heard what you said about email, and I felt myself slinking down in my chair to hide. I am the worst about sending middle-of-the-night emails. I need to change that."

Almost every email application now offers a scheduled send time, so if you want to get that email prepared in the middle of the night, schedule it to go out at the start of contract time the next day. When you send email when you're off the clock, people will assume you are also checking email off the clock, setting an unspoken expectation that you are available during those times.

HAVE A PRE-TYPED RESPONSE TO SEND TO CAREGIVERS ON NIGHTS AND WEEKENDS

While I don't recommend giving caregivers your personal cell number because of the boundary intrusions that tend to occur in this space, I understand that some teachers like to do so or find it necessary based on student and family circumstances. The biggest problem that occurs when caregivers have your personal cell phone number is that they feel more comfortable contacting you during times you're not working.

There is going to be a time when a parent texts and you don't have the desire or bandwidth to respond, but you don't want them to feel ignored. If you have a prepared message in the Notes section of your phone explaining that you will get back to them, it saves a lot of time trying to figure out what to say. Here's a template you can adapt for you:

> *"Hi _____. Thanks for reaching out. I'm with my family right now and not able to chat, but I will get back to you about this tomorrow/on Monday during my conference time. Have a great rest of your night/weekend!"*

Action:
Set Your Communication Expectations

Set up your away and prepared messages in
your email and on your phone.

Chapter Thirteen

WRANGLING IN RUMINATION

"All I can think about is school, even when I'm not at school."

umination

- Lesson plans.
- Progress reports.
- Data collection.
- Tutoring schedules.
- The kid that isn't making progress.
- The parent that just won't stop emailing.
- The administrator who walked in right after you sat down for the first time all day.
- The co-worker you snapped at in a frustrated moment.

The word rumination has two main meanings, but I love how they complement each other to help us understand what psychological rumination means.

Imagine a beautiful green pasture where a cow is feeding on some delicious, fresh grass. That cute little cow swallows the grass, the body digests it a little bit, and then the cow throws up the grass into their mouth to chew some more. This process happens several times before the food is swallowed permanently for digestion.

Psychological rumination is similar in that something negative happens to us that causes emotional distress, and instead of the brain processing it and letting it pass, the brain throws it up again and again and again into the forefront of our mind, especially when we desperately want to stop thinking about it.

Watkins and Roberts (2020) define rumination as "repetitive, prolonged, and recurrent negative thinking about one's self, feelings, personal concerns and upsetting experiences."

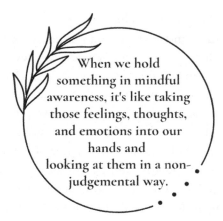

When we hold something in mindful awareness, it's like taking those feelings, thoughts, and emotions into our hands and looking at them in a non-judgemental way.

The difference between our mental process and a cow's digestive process is that cows need this process for their bodies to function correctly, and psychological rumination actually has negative impacts on our body's ability to function properly.

In Watkins and Roberts (2020) review of research, they found that rumination made uncomfortable emotions like sadness, anger, fear, and shame worse, caused people to be less likely to engage in pleasant activities, impaired executive function, increased risk of mental illness, negatively impacted sleep, interfered with the effectiveness of therapy, and kept the sympathetic nervous system revved and stressed, among other things.

One science teacher shared, "When I ruminate, it causes me to make the situation bigger and it makes me have stronger feelings about the situation than I really need to. It negatively impacts my relationships, both with myself and with others because it erodes my confidence, trust, and openness. I get stuck in a cycle of guilt and self doubt and it just goes round and round all day and night. I know the problem needs a solution, but I can't control the thoughts."

This, my dear friends, is what rumination sounds like in real life.

So if we know rumination feels miserable and has negative impacts, what strategies exist to help us learn new ways of coping?

MINDFULNESS PRACTICES

Mindfulness-based cognitive behavioral practices are an evidence-based way to defuse and reduce rumination (Watkins & Roberts, 2020), and mindfulness, as we've discussed in previous chapters, has been proven to be an effective strategy for mitigating burnout in educators (Lukin & Sammons, 2016; Sun et al., 2019; Zarate et al., 2019). The key to mindfulness is being able to step back from the feelings, thoughts, and physical sensations and hold them in mindful awareness. When we hold something in mindful awareness, it's like taking those feelings, thoughts, and emotions into our hands, looking at them in a non-judgmental way, and changing the way we respond, helping our brains re-learn over time how to interact with those thoughts, feelings, and sensations.

THANK YOU MIND

Sometimes when I practice mindful awareness, I imagine my brain is its own entity, separate from myself, and so I talk to my brain like it's my friend, and I keep in mind that this friend, whom I deeply care about, wants to feel emotionally and physically safe. And when I can see my brain and all its thoughts and emotions through the lens of safety, I can recognize why my brain is telling me what it's telling me.

When I taught elementary-aged deaf and hard-of-hearing children, I had a student who had experienced language deprivation (i.e. lack of exposure to language and communication from birth) and, because he couldn't express his basic needs, he got his needs met in unhealthy ways that worked well for him. Sometimes, those unhealthy ways included physically aggressive behaviors that scared me. After some time, I also realized he was being abused at home, and as a survivor of childhood trauma, I felt a strong desire to want to fix the situation for him. I had never worked with a child with this level of challenging behavior, and when I went home at night, I ruminated. I replayed every interaction and every lesson over and over and over, and I was miserable. I lost sleep, my heart was constantly racing thinking about what I needed to do differently, and I felt so much shame, which for me sounded like: *What is wrong with me that I can't figure out how to help this kid?*

What I wish I would've been able to do during these moments was to look at my thoughts without judging them, and to say to my brain, "Thank You Mind" (McKay et al., 2011).

"Thank you mind, for reminding me that I deeply care about this student and want him to feel loved and safe in my classroom."

"Thank you mind, for reminding me that I feel a moral responsibility to help my student learn enough language to report what's happening to him in his home."

MINDFUL SELF-COMPASSION PRACTICE

Another of my favorite practices for rumination, called the Mindful Self-Compassion Practice, was developed by Dr. Kristin Neff, researcher and founder of the Center for Mindful Self Compassion (www.self-compassion.org). To demonstrate this strategy, I'd like to walk you through a short practice right now in the context of your school.

I wonder if you've ever been at work and said something to a fellow teacher or to your principal, and your tone or choice of words left you wishing you hadn't said anything at all. Just tonight, I was having coffee with a long-time mentor, said something with a tone I didn't intend, and then immediately said, "I'm sorry. I didn't mean that the way it sounded."

We are all imperfect humans who make mistakes. Sometimes when we make mistakes, it's hard to let it go. I'm imagining that sometime in the past you said that "thing" or used that "tone" and then went home and spent the evening replaying it over and over in your head and beating yourself up over what you said.

The next time this happens at work, I'd like you to consider talking, thinking, or writing through the following exercise before you go home or as soon as you arrive home, and consider whether you recognize improvement in how much you ruminate that evening.

The mindful self-compassion practice has three components: mindfulness about what happened, recognition of common humanity, and kindness to self (Germer & Neff, 2019).

Step 1: Mindfulness

Write down, think about, or talk with a trusted friend about the difficult experience or the "thing" you feel bad about. Remember how you felt. Be accepting and non-judgmental of those feelings.

Step 2: Acknowledgement

Think about how your experience is connected to a larger experience that all humans/teachers know. Acknowledge underlying causes & conditions.

Step 3: Self-compassion

Think, write, or say kind, understanding words of comfort to yourself.

So for our scenario, that might sound like:

1. Today I was feeling frustrated and made a comment to Sheila in the hallway about being late for morning duty. I wish I had said it with a different tone and in a different way. I wanted her to understand how it impacts me when she's

late, but I went about it in the wrong way. I feel guilty about that. I apologized, but I just feel so bad about it.

2. I know that everyone in the whole world has said things they regret saying when they are feeling frustrated and overwhelmed. I am not the only person who makes this kind of mistake.

3. Oh Jen. You are perfectly imperfect and that is okay. You are doing the best you can with the circumstances of staffing shortages. You are kind in your heart and you made amends. Give yourself a bit of grace, eh? Take a deep breath. Forgive yourself. It's time to go home and enjoy your family.

The next time you've made a mistake and just can't let it go, try a dose of self-compassion and see how it changes your perspective.

Action:
Strategize

What's something you've been ruminating about lately? Pick a strategy to try on for a week and see how it works for you.

For a cheat sheet to help you with Neff's mindful self-compassion practice, go to www.teachercarenetwork.com/book.

Part Four

HARNESS SOCIAL SUPPORT

"Friendship is born at that moment when one person says to another, 'What! You too? I thought I was the only one.' "

— C.S. LEWIS

Social support is a huge strength for many teachers, and simultaneously a concerning weakness. Teachers can't help but bond over hilarious student stories, teaching woes, incredible student progress, and controversial legislation and policies. There are truly things that only another teacher can understand about what it means to be a teacher.

But there are also cultural norms in the profession that don't serve teachers and their mental health well.

In this section of the book, we'll take a look at what we need to start doing and stop doing as we engage social support from co-workers, friends, and family. We'll learn how to look at the social support we have and shape it, through strategies, into a system that supports us in healthy, sustainable ways.

Chapter Fourteen

SUPPORT DURING TIMES OF CRISIS

ack in 1996, teacher burnout was already on the radar of research scientists. Researchers found that having co-worker support buffered emotional exhaustion, decreased depersonalization, and increased feelings of accomplishment (Greenglass et al., 1996; 1997). Translation: Co-worker support reduced symptoms of burnout. Teachers who had support from their co-workers were less exhausted, less emotionally distanced, and felt like they were better teachers.

To illustrate, I want to share a story from a teacher who participates in the Teacher Care Network Support Community.

Imagine adopting two kids through the foster care system, going through a high-risk, unexpected pregnancy, and having a personal health crisis all in the same year - all while being a teacher.

Now imagine going through that experience with high-quality social support that affirms your need for time off to adjust and heal. Imagine co-workers not only covering your teaching load, but also showing up for you personally. This is the kind of support Kandice experienced in 2018 when she had to take a four month leave of absence from her job as an itinerant teacher in deaf education.

Kandice shared:

"In March of 2018, I welcomed 2 boys (6 and 11) into my home through adoption. I immediately took 3 weeks off to adjust and get things set up for them. My team showed up by making sure my students continued to receive services, and they even sent gifts for my boys. One month later, I found myself unexpectedly pregnant with a high-risk pregnancy and my husband had become unemployed. It was rocky, to say the least.

In October, I started a 4 month leave and I felt so supported through all of it by my friends, family, and co-workers. I never had to worry one bit about work during my time off because my team had it taken care of. They planned all the lessons, made sure my caseload was covered, and assessed, planned, and attended all of my students' IEP meetings, all while being supportive of my need to be away.

During that time my youngest son had major surgery out of state. At 30 weeks pregnant, recently diagnosed with gestational diabetes, I spent my 30th birthday at the hospital caring for my son. We arrived to his hospital room and I was surprised with two beautiful floral arrangements from my team. At home, my Dad stayed with my husband and oldest child, working on home improvements to prepare for the baby and helping my oldest while my husband worked. I had support from all directions.

> I had never seen a team show up the way my team did for me. Working in a place with such a high level of social support allows me to fuel my passion for Deaf Education and care for my family simultaneously.

Upon arriving home, I was placed on bed rest, which led to a hospital stay and ultimately my baby being born 4 weeks early. My sweet baby boy was born the day before my planned baby shower. Did we cancel that shower? Of course not! My friends, family, and co-workers still showed up to my shower and I attended via FaceTime while someone else opened my gifts.

On top of all of this, 6 weeks postpartum, I had a severe blood clot in my left leg. My mom stayed with my family for 3 weeks so my husband could work and I could recover. My friends and church family made sure we were fed. My coworkers showed up at my house for two days straight to clean, organize, and stock my fridge! Ultimately, I recovered and returned to work.

I had never seen a team show up the way my team did for me. Working in a place with such a high level of social support allows me to fuel my passion for Deaf Education and care for my family simultaneously. The care for each other helps prevent burnout like nothing I've ever seen."

There are so many nuggets of wisdom we can learn from Kandice's experience. Let's break them down so we can analyze what helped Kandice feel so supported during this crisis.

WORK-RELATED SUPPORTS

When unexpected emergencies happen, it is so important that teachers don't have the weight of preparing weeks upon weeks of lesson plans for their absence. Kandice's team didn't have her plan out 4 months worth of lesson plans for her students. They released her from the burden of work so she could care for herself and her family, and they didn't make her feel guilty about it. They allowed her to prioritize her family, so that when she returned to work, she wasn't resentful of the stress work caused during her time of crisis.

PRACTICAL SUPPORTS

Kandice's team showed up in practical ways. Their support wasn't all work-related all the time. They cleaned. They organized. They stocked her fridge with food to eat to reduce her mental load. They acknowledged her human needs.

Remember my tornado story from chapter 10? My co-workers collected gift cards to help me replace everything I lost, invited me to stay at their houses in guest rooms and on couches, and they fed me dinner almost every night. They did practical things that showed me they cared. This allowed me to show up to work full of gratitude and joy every day in spite of what was going on in my personal life.

SUPPORTS OF KINDNESS

Sometimes acts of pure kindness speak loudly about how much we truly care about an individual when they are going through a hard, or special, time. Showing up for events like baby showers and sending flowers for mourning, well-wishes, or celebration demonstrate that you recognize what is being experienced and want to be part of it.

Action:
Support-Plan in Advance

- Talk with your co-workers about how you will support each other before a crisis happens.
- Discuss what your expectations and your genuine wishes are regarding how to receive support.
- Make commitments and reassure each other that if something happens, you have each other's backs.

Chapter Fifteen

TALKING SHOP

"I never realized how much I talked about work and standardized testing, until my second grader came home at the end of the year and said he was 'done' with school. He had decided he was going to quit school because he didn't want to go to third grade - that's when they start testing."

G retchen and her husband are both teachers who work in a large, Title 1 school in Texas. Their kids are now grown, and she shared that she and her husband have had to set boundaries around how often and how long they talk about work.

"It's not even so much that we talked about students," she said, "we talk about the system and all the ways it's failing, and how it's impacting our students." Gretchen continued, "When I was a kid both my parents worked for the Sheriff's department and they didn't come home and talk about work. I don't know what it is about being in education that causes it." Gretchen described how so much of her identity was being a teacher, it was hard to turn "teacher" off to turn on mom, wife, and friend.

Gretchen described several strategies she and her husband use to manage how much time they spend talking about school at home. When they worked at different campuses, they took turns sharing one thing that happened at work right when they got home. Then they shelved work for the rest of the night. Now that they work at the same campus and ride to and from work together, their conversations about school happen in the car. Once they arrive home, school chatter stops and they focus on their personal lives.

Gretchen described a similar boundary with her best friend, a retired school teacher. They carpool to yoga together each week and on the way to yoga, Gretchen will talk about the latest work news. Then at some point she'll divert the conversation; sometimes she just turns on a song and says "Let's sing!" Then on the way back home from yoga they talk about other things.

I'm feeling so peaceful right now and I want to hold on to that feeling.

Later this summer, Gretchen has a girls trip planned and all of the women attending are current or former teachers. "I already told them I don't want to talk about students or school," she said. "I don't want to talk about anyone else's kids for the whole trip. I want to completely disconnect from work."

Gretchen saw the impact that constantly talking about work had on her relationships, and she made sustainable changes. When I asked teachers in the Teacher Care Network Support Community what they do to limit "shop talk," they shared similar strategies that all came down to setting boundaries.

SET BOUNDARIES AROUND TOPICS

What are the topics that really get you wound up as an educator? Funding? School violence? Standardized testing?

On days when you are struggling or on days where you feel good and want to keep it that way, it's okay to say, "I don't want to talk about _____ today." No explanation is required when you set a boundary, and if asked, you can simply respond, "Because I prefer it that way."

SET BOUNDARIES AROUND EVENTS/LOCATIONS

Where are the places you go that you want to protect from "shop talk?"

For my husband and me, it's date nights and late nights. If we have a night away from our toddler or have some time together after our toddler goes to bed, we suspend all talk about work unless it's something that really needs to be discussed because it impacts the family.

If you are from a family of educators, you might have to set limits around "shop talk" for holidays or dinner out. That could sound like, "I'd like to request that we don't talk about work at dinner tonight because I really want to connect personally," or "I'd like to wait to talk about work until after the cookout." Sometimes I'll add something like, "I'm feeling so peaceful right now and I want to hold on to that feeling."

SET BOUNDARIES AROUND TIME

Gretchen and her husband choose to talk about work during their commute because it's relatively short - 10 minutes from their home to their school. If you don't commute with your friend or family member, you might have to set a more obvious boundary. That might mean setting a timer or just being mindful of the need to share and move on.

HAVE NON-EDUCATOR FRIENDS IN YOUR LIFE

If you find it difficult to set boundaries with educator friends, make friends with people who aren't educators. When I was a special education teacher my best friend worked for a roofer. She didn't know anything about public schools. She couldn't engage in an in-depth conversation with me about work because she didn't understand my work well enough to do so.

She also saw the bottom line a lot more clearly than my educator friends did because she wasn't in the problem with me. I could talk to an educator friend about something that happened at work, and we could go back and forth for hours with stories and lamenting.

I could call her afterwards and tell the same story and within 5 minutes she'd say something like, "So it sounds like you didn't feel respected as a professional."

I'd respond with "Yeah, I guess not," and somehow that meaning she helped me make was enough to help me move forward.

She couldn't share a similar story because she didn't have one. All she could do is listen well to the general arc of the story and think of how that related to what she knew of me personally.

This is the power of a friend outside of the profession. They don't know you as a fellow teacher or colleague. They don't know your work world. They just know YOU.

Action:

Think About - Write About - Talk About

Reflect on your tendency to talk "shop."
• How does "shop talk" impact your relationships?
• Do you want to set boundaries?
• With whom?
• Under what circumstances?
• What would that look like for you?
• Do you have relationships with non-educators?
• Do you want or need more?
• What can you do to make that happen?

Chapter Sixteen

SUPPORT FROM THE BROADER COMMUNITY

O ur opportunities for connection have blossomed with the advent of the Internet, but especially social media. Even since the pandemic began, the accessibility of community has grown. When people couldn't meet face to face, they invented and adapted, and the amount of support available online has skyrocketed as a result.

Everywhere you look, there are opportunities for teachers to meet together in virtual spaces to discuss what's going on in their school and get support from fellow teachers. Some of these spaces are helpful, some harmful, but there are certainly an array of options.

A few years ago, I didn't see the value of online support spaces quite yet. I questioned how they could be effective and whether they could be healthy, functional spaces that facilitate being seen, heard, valued, and supported. I wondered if true relationships could be built, or if the space would simply serve as a container for negativity. I saw toxicity happening in unmonitored spaces, and I was skeptical about how it could be a positive space for growth.

So, in alignment with my love of educational psychology, I dug into the research, and it did not say what I thought it would say. That's the beauty of science and research, isn't it?

In a review of literature, researchers found that the use of Facebook to access social support improved health outcomes in the areas of mental health, physical health, well-being, and reducing mental illness symptomology (Gilmour et al., 2020). In a study specific to the teaching profession, Chung and Chen (2018) found social support via Facebook improved self-efficacy, indicating that teachers are not exempt from the benefits of online social support.

My first reaction was "Wait a minute! I've heard social media is bad for mental health. What am I missing?!"

By further looking into the research, I uncovered that using social media for social support is markedly different than using social media for general use; using social media for general purposes is associated with negative mental health outcomes (Frost & Rickwood, 2017).

In essence, going to social media without a purpose, scrolling, and randomly interacting is not beneficial. However, going to social media for a purpose, to seek quality social support, has strong benefits.

Going to social media without a purpose, scrolling, and randomly interacting is not beneficial. However, going to social media for a purpose, to seek quality social support, has strong benefits.

So what does quality social support look like? How do you decide if a social media support group is healthy and good for you? Here are a couple of things to consider when deciding if an online support space is safe and right for you:

LOGISTICS OF SAFE SOCIAL SUPPORT SPACES

- Does the space have active moderators/facilitators that are invested in the group remaining a safe space for people to gather?
- Are there explicit group guidelines posted so expectations around appropriate and inappropriate interaction are clear?
- Are guidelines enforced equitably by moderators?
- Is the space a closed space, meaning some form of vetting is required before a new member is admitted?

EMOTIONAL SAFETY OF SUPPORT SPACES

- Do you feel dread or anxiety about what you may read in the space?
- Do you feel supported when you post a question?
- Even if you don't receive a straightforward answer to your question, do you feel seen and heard when you share?
- Does visiting the group and reading its threads/posts induce anxiety or anger?
- Do you feel reasonably safe to say what is so for you in the group?

Remain in groups that are logistically and emotionally safe and leave groups that are not.

Action:
Join the Community

I created the Teacher Care Network
Support Community based on best practices
for online support communities. It is free
and closely moderated. I encourage you to
join to check it out. You can always leave,
and you're always welcomed back.

You can find links to the groups for teachers
and administrators at:
www.teachercarenetwork.com/book.

Chapter Seventeen

THE VALUE OF VENTING

"I just need to vent."

How many times have you said that phrase or heard someone else say it? Probably a lot. It's a phrase that we use a lot in our culture and in the teaching profession.

Something happens that doesn't feel good. We want relief, compassion, and understanding, so we seek out someone to hear our story. We recount what happened with all the nitty gritty details and how we felt about it.

I don't know about you, but it never seems like enough. I want to tell another person and another person and another person, depending on how upset I am.

Physiologically, what's happening is that, every time I tell the story, my body is re-experiencing it, as if it's happening again. My body is flooding itself with stress hormones again, and instead of feeling better, I feel worse. For example, if I have an incident with a student, and a few hours later I verbally recall what happened, my body doesn't really understand that the event has passed.

In cases of trauma, there have long been concerns about re-victimizing survivors by requiring them to retell what happened, and there is much literature and study of revictimization. When we vent, we experience something similar on a smaller scale. As I'm venting about what happened, and recalling how I felt, I may start to experience the same symptoms I experienced when it was happening. Maybe I feel my face flush or I notice I'm sweating. Perhaps my anxiety increases and I feel heat shoot throughout my body. Maybe I notice my feelings of anger or sadness rise up again.

So if venting isn't helpful, what's the alternative? How can we engage social support without telling our stories?

The answer isn't to stop sharing our stories, but to change how we share and how we interact with the sharing of stories.

> The answer isn't to stop sharing our stories, but to change how we share and how we interact with the sharing of stories.

Lee and colleagues (2020) analyzed the conversations of 168 people who were in the middle of a conflict with someone and were still upset about it. Researchers split the group in two and had conversations with the participants about what had happened. First they asked participants: "How do you feel right now on a scale of 1 to 100?" Half of the participants were asked questions that guided them to recount, or vent, about what happened. Half of the participants were asked questions that guided them to reconstrue what happened. To reconstrue is to make meaning of your experience. They rated the intensity of their emotions and physical reactions as they were having the conversation.

Then they were asked again, "How do you feel right now on a scale of 1 to 100?"

People who were led to recount, or vent about, their experience showed a significant increase in negative affect (feelings/emotions). People who were led to reconstrue their experience were protected against an increase in negative affect and reported feelings of closure.

So the grand question is – what were the differences in the questions they were asked? What is the difference between recounting and reconstruing?

PARTICIPANTS WHO RECOUNTED, OR VENTED ABOUT, THEIR EXPERIENCES WERE ASKED:

1. Can you tell me about what happened—what happened and what did you feel—from start to finish?
2. What went through your mind during the exact moment?
3. What stuck out the most at that moment?
4. What did (he/she/they) say and do?
5. How did this make you feel at that moment?

PARTICIPANTS WHO RECONSTRUED WERE ASKED:

1. Looking at the situation, could you tell me why this event was stressful to you?
2. Why do you think you reacted to (the event/the person) that way?
3. Why do you think (the other person in your experience) reacted that way?
4. Have you learned anything from this experience, and if so, would you mind sharing it with me?
5. In the grand scheme of things, if you look at the "big picture," does that help you make sense of this experience? Why or why not?

I want to be clear that I'm not suggesting that you never recount an experience. There are situations where recounting what happened is necessary and helpful, especially when we need intervention from another person to help us. What I am suggesting instead is that you become aware of times when recounting may not benefit you, and use a tool to process the experience that does benefit you.

When I first ran into this research and decided to try out reconstruing for myself, I started by using the guiding questions as a journal prompt. When I found myself wanting to go vent to my partner or a friend, I told myself, "You can go vent after you've answered these questions."

I didn't want to take venting away from myself, because that seemed like an extreme shift. I just wanted to try something new and see how it impacted my internal need to vent.

Sometimes, I found I didn't feel the need to vent after I journaled through the questions, and other times I still had a felt need to talk to someone. What I changed was how I approached the conversation. I gave a brief description of what happened, and jumped right into discussing what I had journaled about, which was driven by those prompts to reconstrue.

This might look different for you. You might just think through the questions instead of journaling about it. You might engage a coworker to commit to the process and ask each other the questions the next time you need to vent. You might type out the answers to the questions on your computer or phone. It doesn't really matter how you integrate the guiding questions or that you use them forever and for every situation. They are simply a tool to help you learn to "vent" differently in a way that benefits you the most.

Action:
Don't Recount, Reconstrue

The next time you find yourself itching to vent, try using the reconstruing guiding questions, and see if you feel a difference.

Part Five

TEND TO YOURSELF

"When we actually do the work of taking the time to tune ourselves, as if we were a precious instrument within a robust orchestra, everyone benefits."

— JENNIFER WOLKIN, PHD, *QUICK CALM*

When I was a kid, I had certain ideas about what it would be like to be an adult. "I'm gonna do what I want, when I want, and it's gonna be so easy." I thought ice cream for breakfast and kicking soccer balls in the house were going to be life-changing when I became a grown-up. I think it came down to feeling like I had no power and control over my environment.

Then I arrived in adulthood and realized that being an adult is ridiculously hard work, and I still don't have as much power and control over my environment as I'd like!

My to-do list seems never-ending. Someone is always vying for my attention. And I am tired of deciding what to eat three times a day! Who's with me?

Just caring for myself seems like such an insurmountable task at times. I'm thankful that I've been able to dig into science to figure out strategies and rhythms to help me so that I can share them with you.

I want to ask you to stick with me through the last few chapters of this book. They are going to sound and feel very "self-care"-ish and I know that is a triggering concept for many of you after years of having "self-care" shoved down your throat and thrown at you like a big bandaid for real emotional and physical exhaustion.

I promise you, this is not a bandaid attempt. This part of the book is all about getting realistic and honest about what we can do to care for ourselves in ways that are sustainable, compassionate, and effective. Think of each chapter like a workshop, where you will read information and then have resources and prompts to implement the information in practical ways.

There is no pressure to do anything that doesn't serve you. There is no shame in saying "no thank you" to practices that don't work for you. You are in control of the process, and you get to decide what to embrace and what to set aside. You get to decide what practices will help you grow so you can thrive in the way you imagine.

Chapter Eighteen

DITCHING SHAME & CREATING PLEASURE

Obligations. *Ugh.*

When I read, write, or say that word, I have quite a visceral reaction in my body. My first thought - without even knowing what the obligation is: "I don't want to. Nope. Not doing it!"

Now there are some obligations that I don't love, but I do them because there are massive consequences for not doing them. For example, I'm not a fan of shelling out a nice sum of money for my mortgage every month, but if I don't fulfill my obligations, the bank takes my house, and I don't have a place to live, so I'm pretty motivated to prioritize that obligation because the consequences are extreme.

Then there are obligations that have less extreme consequences in the short term, so if I don't do it, nobody really knows except me - at least that's what I tell myself. For example, when I hear people talk about self-care, and say "You need to [blah, blah, blah]," I feel like someone else is trying to pour expectations and shame over my very tired mind and body, so I tell myself, "I don't have time to be mindful about what I eat or to go to therapy - *AND YOU CAN'T MAKE ME!*"

Any other "you can't make me" folks out there? Just me?

I have struggled with shaming obligation messages around "taking care of myself" for as long as I can remember. When I was a teen, my mom used to use a shaming tone of voice and say, "Jennifer, you *really* need to shave your legs." While I knew that was something I needed to do because it was a cultural expectation, and maybe even wanted to do sometimes, just the fact that my mother mentioned it and made it sound like I had an obligation to do it made me dig my heels in and refuse. I was the junior high girl leading "no-shave challenges" to see who could grow the longest leg hair - all because I felt like I was being sold a shaming obligation message.

> If we can replace that obligation message with something else - something that feels good - then we're more likely to do the "things" we need to do to care for ourselves.

What I have realized over the past 10 years, as I've tried strategy after strategy to defeat my own shaming thought process about obligatory "self-care," is that I can't win the obligation shame game.

If I view something as a shame-filled obligation, there is no strategy I have found that will change my mind or actions in the long-term. When I talk to teachers about taking care of themselves, I hear similar stories that lead me to believe that I'm not the only one with this particular struggle.

When we view something as an obligation, it tends to create an emotional cocktail of anger or resentment (that we have to do it in the first place), guilt (when we don't do it), and more shame (when we feel our inability to get it done is a personal defect).

If we can replace that obligation message with something else - something that feels good - then we're more likely to do the "things" we need to do to care for ourselves.

For me, it's pleasure. When something feels like an obligation – causing me to dig my heels in – I have to figure out how to make that thing I need to do into something that feels good.

My mom passed away this year, and in the last month of her life, I was providing care in awkward shifts of time and in places – like hospitals far from where I live – that were not conducive to basic care of my body. I went days without brushing my teeth without even realizing it was happening.

Then, after my mom passed, I just couldn't get back into the habit of brushing my teeth. Teeth brushing has always been unpleasant for me, and I really resented my husband and my therapist telling me that it's something I needed to do, even though I knew it was true! I poured shame over my own head with thoughts like, "What is wrong with me that I can't just brush my teeth like everyone else?!"

What ended up helping me get back in the habit of brushing was removing the shame-filled obligation message and replacing it with a routine that felt good for me. Now I turn on music while I brush, and take deep breaths. I look at myself in the eyes in the mirror and tell myself how proud I am of myself for doing it. And I purposefully brush at the same time as my toddler, because what is more fun than watching a 3 year old pretend to be a lion while they brush!

I'm wondering what shame-filled obligation messages you're carrying around on your back that are causing you to not do the things you really want to do to care for yourself?

Action:
Transform Obligations into Options

Make a T-chart. On the left, list one obligation message you've received about taking care of yourself. On the right, jot down some ideas that could make that care task feel good and pleasurable.

Action bonus:
Think About - Talk About - Write About

• Do you dread taking care of yourself?
• Do you avoid it?
• What would need to change for you to experience pleasure from taking care of yourself?

Chapter Nineteen

TIME-BLOCKING CARE

"I don't have time to take care of myself."

I wonder if this is something you have said or thought? If you have, you're not alone. I cannot count the times I've seen a social media post about teacher self-care, looked in the comments, and saw this phrase over and over and over.

And it resonates with me too. When I was in the classroom, I was exhausted and had no tools to help me figure out how to care for myself.

The last time a teacher said this to me in a workshop, I followed that statement with, "Are you interested in considering a way of taking care of yourself that doesn't require you to create more time?"

I got the cynical, "Suuuure. Ooookay."

You might still be feeling that cynicism right now!

I want to share some hope as we hop into a few chapters on caring for ourselves.

Recently, that cynical teacher from that workshop emailed me after a couple of weeks of implementing time-blocked care and said, "This is literally changing my life!"

I can't promise this chapter and the next few are going to change your life, but I'm pretty confident they're going to get you moving in a sustainable direction that feels functional and good in your mind and body.

Are you interested in considering a way of taking care of yourself that doesn't require you to create more time?

Caring for ourselves doesn't usually make the daily or weekly "to-do list" unless it's an appointment of some kind, and frankly the most sustainable forms of care aren't done at appointments. We'll get into types of care in the next couple of chapters, but for now, I just want to focus on two aspects of time that help us think about care in a different way: a macro-view, and a micro-view.

I want you to do a quick visualization of the timeline of the year. Zoom out from the day you're experiencing, and see the big picture. Maybe you visualize your year on a big, 12-month paper calendar, or maybe you visualize the year on a single timeline with major events marked, such as "First Day of School" or "Winter Break" or "My Birthday." That's your macro-view of time.

Now I want you to imagine zooming in on a specific day in your calendar or timeline. If I zoom in on July 4, I might see a day off of work where I sleep in, have a leisurely breakfast, spend some time with my partner and son, then join my extended family at my dad's house for a cook-out and sparklers. That's my micro-view of time.

When we plan for care of any kind, we need to have both views of time in mind. We need to know how care will look from a 30,000 ft level flying through the year, and how it will look as we are touching down each day. We do that by thinking critically about care activities that happen annually, monthly, weekly, and daily. Then we zoom in even closer and decide how we will practice care within our day in 1 minute, 5 minute, 15 minute, and 30+ minute increments.

At first glance, I know that may sound overwhelming, but I'm going to walk you through this process over the next couple of chapters, and by the end of those short chapters, you're going to have the start of a robust, reasonable, sustainable plan for caring for yourself within the time limitations that already exist in your day to day life.

Action:
Prepare for Organized Care

Today's only task is to download the worksheets we're going to be using to organize our care plan starting tomorrow. You can download these on my website: www.teachercarenetwork.com/book

Chapter Twenty

PHYSICAL CARE

Out of all of the areas of caring for ourselves, physical care seems to get the most attention, and because of that, when we think about caring for ourselves, physical care tasks are usually what come to mind. I think about things like showering, eating nutritious food, exercising, taking my medications and supplements, and stuff like that.

If I'm honest, it's my least favorite of the six areas of care because our culture has such shaming messages around what physical care should look like and be like.

I've dreaded writing this chapter because I want it to be helpful, non-shaming, and life-giving. I knew that was going to take some real word-smithing and deep thought and consideration of how every sentence will be received by those who struggle with physical care, or who are assumed to struggle with physical care because of their size or disability.

As a "plus-size" woman with chronic illness, I have often felt shamed by doctors, family, friends, memes, and department stores about the body I live in. I find that people and institutions make assumptions about what physical care I do or don't do, and what relationship that has to my body size and type.

I'm not here to judge what you do or don't do as it relates to phys-ical care. I just want to help you think about what physical care you WANT to do, and how to make that work for you.

Let's work through a couple of areas of physical care to get you thinking about your macro- and micro-care needs.

If you need extra ideas, there's a thread in the Teacher Care Network Support Community where teachers share what is on their list.

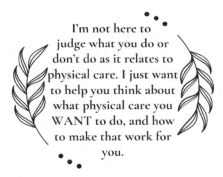

I'm not here to judge what you do or don't do as it relates to physical care. I just want to help you think about what physical care you WANT to do, and how to make that work for you.

ANNUAL PHYSICAL CARE

When I think about the necessity of planning for annual care tasks, I think about the scary fact that I once went a couple of years without a well-woman exam because I never got around to it. I started having pain in my breast, made an appointment, and realized at that appoint-ment (because they mentioned it repeatedly) that it had been almost three years since I had been to the gynecologist.

Given the history of cancer in my family and my desire to be a generally healthy woman, this was a wake up call for me. Thankfully, it ended up being a benign area, but I realized at that time I needed to start having a list of annual tasks.

For me, these annual tasks are things like getting a well-woman exam, participating in open enrollment so I make sure I get the health insurance plan that meets my family's needs, and changing my tooth-brush twice!

What are the tasks you want on *your* list?

MONTHLY OR BI-WEEKLY PHYSICAL CARE

These are care tasks that happen more frequently, but still not frequently enough that you can easily forget. When was the last time you were in the shower and realized, "UGH, I'm out of shampoo."

Are you the kind of person who adds the water and shakes it to use the very last drop? I used to be, and not because I was trying to not be wasteful, but because I had no other option!

What about refilling prescriptions? Any last-minute refillers reading these pages? There are so many moments of emotional frustration that can be avoided if we have planned physical care in advance.

On the top of my list are tending to prescriptions, purchasing care products, and getting my legs waxed! Remember that junior high girl running those no-shave challenges? It turns out I just really don't like taking long showers, and shaving takes time. My grown-up solution? I just get my legs waxed once a month and then I'm done! Don't be afraid of trying a new strategy or taking a shortcut if you can think of one.

WEEKLY PHYSICAL CARE

Weekly physical care tasks are the gray space between daily tasks and bi-weekly or monthly tasks. These might be tasks you do once a week or a few times a week. For example, I refill my pill organizer once a week. That's on my weekly care task list. I go to yoga between 2 and 5 times a week, but not daily, so that also goes on my weekly care task list.

When I was developing this system originally for myself, I started to feel uncomfortable when I got to the weekly tasks. I felt particularly 'ugh' because I knew exercise should go on my list, but it felt icky putting it on there because I was so exhausted and I didn't want to commit to doing something I knew I couldn't do. I didn't want to pile any more guilt or shame on myself, so I changed the word "exercise" to "enjoyable movement." I could commit to "enjoyable movement" when I couldn't commit to exercise.

Remember that chapter on turning shame-filled obligation to pleasure? This is a prime example.

The same concept applies to nutrition. As a busy mom + educational psychologist, I cannot commit to cooking full meals every day of the week. I also can't commit to meal prepping every week. It works great for some people; it hasn't worked for me yet. It might work great for you! We are individuals with individual needs. What I settled on for my needs was having balanced, quick food options available in a variety of forms: fresh, frozen, pre-prepared, needs preparation.

When you're considering your weekly tasks, don't get caught up in the "shoulds." *I should do this. I should do that.* Focus on what you truly want for yourself.

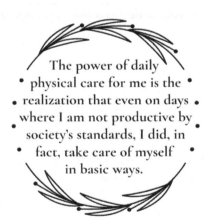

The power of daily physical care for me is the realization that even on days where I am not productive by society's standards, I did, in fact, take care of myself in basic ways.

DAILY PHYSICAL CARE

At the bare minimum, most of us are doing some kind of grooming care tasks and eating daily. I think the power of listing these out is to give yourself credit for the care you are probably already doing every day without fail.

Most days you brush your teeth. Most days you brush your hair. Most days you have a few meals.

Sometimes I get to the end of the day and declare, "I didn't get anything done today," and then I feel ashamed. Do you know that feeling?

The power of daily physical care for me is the realization that even on days where I am not productive by society's standards, I did, in fact, take care of myself in basic ways.

As you move forward with making your list of physical care tasks, I want you to note beside each care task the amount of time it will take to complete. See if you can think of tasks that give you quick 30-second and 10-minute wins! Those are sometimes the hardest to think of, but they give us the quickest return. We will come back to time-blocking our care in chapter 23 when we are putting everything together. Don't forget to include tasks that close the stress response cycle from chapter 5.

Action:
Think About - Talk About - Write About

For physical care, brainstorm ideas for annual, monthly, weekly, and daily tasks.

Chapter Twenty-One

EMOTIONAL & PSYCHOLOGICAL CARE

W hen I was growing up, emotional and psychological care were not emphasized in any of the spaces I frequented. We didn't talk about it at school. We didn't talk about it at home. And we certainly didn't talk about it at church unless it was tied to a discussion about how emotions can make you sin.

Even into my early '20s, I had no concept of what mental health really encompassed. I had some exposure to mental illness because my grandmother had a mental illness that impaired her ability to maintain relationships and employment, but mental *health* wasn't even on my radar.

I started going to counseling regularly my first year of teaching. At that point in my life, I had been carrying around a secret for over a decade: that I had experienced childhood sexual abuse. One of the devastating things caused by childhood abuse is a perception that you were older and more responsible than you actually were at the time you were abused. My abuse experiences occurred around age 8, and I had in my mind what 8 year olds look like, and what they are capable of understanding.

When I became a teacher of 8 year olds, my whole conceptualization of my role in my experience of abuse blew up.

I vividly remember sitting at my desk in my first classroom looking at the clock. It was about 7:55. Students were going to be entering my classroom in less than 5 minutes, and I felt like my internal world was imploding. I quickly Googled "counselor near McKinney," clicked on the first name, and immediately scheduled an intake appointment. The date of my first counseling appointment was September 18, 2009. I celebrate that date as my "counsel-versary" because the process that began that day completely changed the course of my life.

I reflect with compassion, and dream with abandon.

It sparked my interest in child abuse prevention, challenging behavior, and eventually teacher emotional health. Thirteen years later, I'm an educational psychologist who specializes in emotional health and safety, and it all started with an intuitive and urgent decision to see a therapist years ago.

I wonder what your experience was with mental health when you were growing up. Did you learn what it meant to take good care of your emotional and psychological self? If you're like me and you didn't learn, or you're always interested in learning new strategies, I want to give you a couple of ideas to help you develop a robust set of emotional and psychological care practices that will help your heart and soul bloom. This set of practices is by no means exhaustive, but it will give you a good place to start.

IDEAS FOR ANNUAL CARE TASKS

Screenings

If you are not currently under the care of a licensed counselor or psychiatrist, the most important annual care task is to get a mental health screening. Mental health check-ups have yet to become routine in most healthcare systems, but there are some doctors who now routinely include depression and anxiety screenings in the paperwork their patients complete annually. If your physician doesn't include mental health screening, ask to be screened or complete a self-screening online. You can find a variety of self-screeners available through Mental Health America at https://screening.mhanational.org/.

Vacations and Time Away

Many people enjoy the benefits of an annual vacation as part of their emotional and psychological care plans. Vacations don't have to be elaborate to be effective. In fact, a vacation is just time spent outside of the normal environment for the purpose of pleasure. Studies have shown that vacations can reduce stress, burnout, exhaustion and absenteeism (Chen & Petrick, 2013). Passive activities, savoring, and pleasure from activities, relaxation, control, and sleep provide the most significant impacts on health and wellness during long summer vacations (de Bloom, 2012), but the catch is that positive effects of taking a vacation fade at various rates.

While many people feel subjective increases in well-being, the positive impacts don't last forever (Chen & Petrick, 2013). This is why summer breaks away from teaching do not cure burnout. Regardless, a good vacation provides a much needed opportunity for psychological detachment.

Each year, my family takes a simple, low-cost vacation, usually to an AirBnB with beautiful scenery. We spend our time savoring and slowing and enjoying nature. Sometimes we take a walk or drive to a look-out. Sometimes we spend all day sitting on a porch. Other families love adventure-filled vacations and theme parks or traveling to exotic locations. Whatever you do, the important part isn't where you go, it's that you allow yourself to connect with yourself and your loved ones, sip your coffee a little slower than normal, and bask in the moment.

I also take a solo trip annually to really think deeply about how I'm doing at treating myself like a human and also how I'm serving the world through my skills as an educational psychologist. I reflect with compassion, and dream with abandon. I think about what is working, and what I'd like to change about how I'm showing up at home and in my profession, and I think about my personal and professional goals. Before I could afford an annual getaway for just me, I would travel to a friend's house and use a spare bedroom. I'd go stay with family and get away to a coffee shop during the day. Whatever works for you, your flow, and your resources is best.

> In the busyness of life, we have a tendency to keep pushing forward day after day without stopping and really thinking about how we're doing.

IDEAS FOR WEEKLY OR BI-WEEKLY CARE TASKS

Intentionally Connect in a Close Relationship.

Researchers have described close friendships as "vaccines" against mental and physical illness and "buffers" of how we respond to life stressors (Sias & Bartoo, 2007; Turner & Brown, 2010).

Quality friendships also increase our experience of happiness (Sanchez et al., 2020). Who is that person in your life that loves you well, supports you through thick and thin, and always has your back? Some people name their spouse or significant other. Others name a best friend. Only you know who that person is for you. Spending time with that person in a setting where you can really connect deeply on what's been going on in your life is key to emotional health.

Check In With Yourself About Your Overall Well-Being

Sometimes when I meet for the first time with teachers who are struggling with burnout symptoms, they say things like, "I don't know what happened! I was fine, and then I wasn't."

In the busyness of life, we have a tendency to keep pushing forward day after day without stopping and really thinking about how we're doing.

There are lots of ways to engage in an intentional "self check in." It doesn't have to look a certain way. I personally like to go sit in a coffee shop, or outside on my back porch, with my journal out and my phone and computer put away, and just think and write about what comes up. I try to do this once a week. That may not be your style of checking in. Maybe you need to take a morning to go fishing or take a walk around the neighborhood. Maybe just lying in bed on Saturday mornings and intentionally thinking about your well-being works great for you.

Here are some questions I ask myself. You can use these or develop your own based on your needs.

- Am I showing up at work how I want to show up?
- Am I showing up at home how I want to show up?
- What went well this week?
- What is there to celebrate?
- What would I like to be different?
- If I had one "do-over" from the past week, what would it be?

Mental Health Counseling or Coaching

After conducting your annual mental health screening or doing your self check-in, you may realize you are experiencing a problem that requires assistance from a professional. One of the most common questions people ask me is about the difference in mental health counseling and coaching. I want to break that down for you so you can make an informed decision that best meets your needs.

Mental health counselors are trained to diagnose and treat mental illnesses based on the DSM-V medical model. Much of their work focuses on "ameliorating pain, understanding symptoms, accepting oneself, resolving conflict (internal and external), and thinking about the past ('rear view mirror') and feelings" (Gooding, 2003).

Coaches lead clients through a process that helps them set goals, make plans to take action, and use their natural strengths to make better decisions that move them forward. Much of their work is focused on "empowerment, values, wants, desires, and visions of the future and the action to make those visions happen" (Gooding, 2003).

I have personally used both mental health counselors and coaches in my journey of developing sustainable energy, connection, and joy. Both fields have a lot to offer teachers who are recovering from burnout.

You can find a directory of mental health counselors at www.psychologytoday.com. For more information about burnout-related coaching, go to my website at www.teachercarenetwork.com.

IDEAS FOR DAILY CARE TASKS

Breathwork Exercises

I started learning more about the science of breathwork when I decided to give restorative yoga a try as a way of intentionally relaxing. I had always encouraged clients and students to use breathing as a calming strategy, but I became particularly interested in using elongated exhalation when I tried it in yoga and literally felt my body hit the stress breaks. I wanted to know what was scientifically happening in my brain, so I went to the literature. Scientists found that breathing in for 4 seconds, followed by breathing out for 6 seconds activates the parasympathetic nervous system (Komori, 2018). The parasympathetic nervous system is the system that tells our body we are safe and can return to a state of calm after an experience of stress.

So when you're feeling stress in your body, breathing out longer than you breathe in is an excellent strategy to help your body shift from fight or flight to rest and digest. You can find more breathwork exercises on my blog at www.teachercarenetwork.com/blog.

Expressing Emotions

When you feel something happening inside your body and mind, stop and pay attention to it. Hold it in mindful awareness, not judging its reason for existing. Then do something with the feeling.

If you're happy, stay with the feeling as long as you can.
If you're sad, experience the loss.
If you're angry, affirm the injustice.
If you're hurt, seek comfort.
If you're afraid, move to safety.
Laugh. Talk. Cry. Create. Breathe. Feel. Express.

Engage in Resting, Savoring, and Time Travel

In the hustle and bustle of daily teacher life, sometimes we forget to slow down, rest, and enjoy the simple things about our lives.

Resting could mean as much as a two hour nap, or as little as putting your head down on your desk for a minute. It could mean sitting in your car for 5 minutes after you arrive home just to relax before you go in the house to be with your family. Maybe you give yourself permission to sleep in on a weekend or just sit in the park without an agenda for an hour on a Saturday afternoon. Make small, intentional choices to rest.

Savoring occurs when we pay attention to pleasant experiences in the moment, and when we savor, we experience positive emotions more frequently and at a higher intensity (Erisman & Roemer, 2010; Quoidbach et al., 2010). In other words, when we experience something that feels good, we stop and notice it and we intentionally try to stay with that feeling longer. Focus on enjoying eating delicious food. Stop and acknowledge how the warmth of the sun feels on your skin. Sit with the feelings of goodness when you experience them.

Positive Mental Time Travel sounds a bit kooky, but it's an evidence-based way to predict happiness.

When we "time travel" in our minds, we vividly remember or anticipate positive experiences (Quoidbach et al., 2010). Research shows that reminiscing twice a day for 10 minutes about past positive experiences increases happiness over the course of the week (Bryant et al., 2005). This ties in really well with building compassion satisfaction, where we intentionally document positive feelings and experiences at work so we can look back on them and remember.

Don't limit yourself to work, though! Take moments each day to think about great things that have happened in your life. If you struggle thinking of positive past experiences in the moment, start a Note in your phone and make a list until you get used to the practice.

As you move forward with making your list of emotional care tasks, note beside each care task the amount of time it will take to complete. See if you can think of tasks that give you quick 30-second and 10-minute wins! Those are sometimes the hardest to think of, but they give us the quickest return.

Don't forget to include strategies you learned from other parts of the book, such as psychological detachment and compassion satisfaction strategies. We will come back to time-blocking our care in chapter 23 when we are putting everything together.

Action:
Think About - Talk About - Write About

For emotional/psychological care, brainstorm ideas for annual, monthly, weekly, and daily task.

Chapter Twenty-Two

OTHER WAYS TO CARE

There are four other areas of care that have either been covered in depth in other parts of the book or require less in-depth explanation. As you work through each area of care, stop and complete the brainstorming and planning questions.

It's okay if you don't get through this chapter in one day. Just because the area of care doesn't require a long explanation doesn't mean that it will be easy to determine what you want and need for that area of your life. Give yourself the grace to move slowly and meaningfully through each section.

PROFESSIONAL CARE

When I talk about taking good care of our professional selves, I often get cynical looks from the audience.

Professional care means a variety of things across the literature, but when I talk about professional care, I define it as all of the tasks and activities we participate in that help us perform well and feel good about our work. This could include tasks like completing your lesson plans by a certain time every week to reduce your weekend stress, or attending a conference each year that gives you fresh ideas that bring you excitement about what's to come.

Sometimes teachers tell me they choose to work a few hours on the weekend (see chapter 11 for a strategy) because they know it will help their week go more smoothly. Often teachers mention it to me because they feel guilty for choosing to work. Reframing the choice to work at home as professional care helps teachers see their choice in a different way that leads to more acceptance and less resentment of their need to feel competent and prepared at work.

- What do you do annually to engage in professional care?
- Are there any tasks you complete monthly to help you feel more prepared for work?
- What tasks do you complete weekly that keep your week on track?
- Do you have any daily rituals related to your work?

FINANCIAL CARE

It's no secret that teachers are underpaid, and I don't have grand solutions for fixing that problem that haven't already been discussed extensively elsewhere. Finances are not my expertise, and I don't have any groundbreaking ideas for making money stretch. There are other professionals with excellent strategies for that. What I do know is that having a financial care plan helps me know **when** I need to do **what** to keep me on target. Here are some questions to consider as you develop your care plan:

- What financial activities do you need to complete annually? (e.g. taxes)
- Is there anything you do monthly to help you stay on track financially? (e.g. confirm expenditures to catch fraud or identity theft)
- Are there weekly tasks that help you stay on top of your finances? (e.g. comparing budget to expenditures to prevent overspending)

- What do you do daily to take care of your finances? (e.g. always put your card back in your wallet to prevent loss)

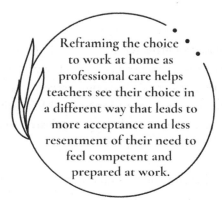

Reframing the choice to work at home as professional care helps teachers see their choice in a different way that leads to more acceptance and less resentment of their need to feel competent and prepared at work.

SPIRITUAL CARE

Spiritual care encompasses nurturing our souls and finding our place within a world that is larger than ourselves. For some people, this involves religion, but it doesn't have to. Scientists have found through empirical study that spiritual experiences benefit both religious and non-religious people by inducing experiences of awe through a perception of the self as small, whether in relation to God, to nature, or to a hero (Preston & Shin, 2017).

Spiritual care could include intentional practices such as self-reflection, being out in nature, volunteering in your community, or gathering with people with similar beliefs. Consider these guiding questions as you contemplate what spiritual practices you might integrate into your life:

- What can you do annually to connect to your spiritual self?
- What would you like to do on a monthly basis to incorporate spiritual care into your life?
- Are there weekly practices that would help you connect spiritually?

- What daily practices would help you experience a sense of inner peace?

SOCIAL CARE

Even though we had an entire section of the book on social support, I wanted to include this here because social support takes effort and planning. As a critical aspect of burnout prevention, taking good care of our social selves requires intentionality and forethought. Consider these guiding questions, and don't forget the strategies from Part 4 - Harness Social Support:

- What annual commitments do I want to make to ensure I receive social support throughout the year?
- What can I do monthly to provide myself with social support?
- What do I need on a weekly basis from people around me, and how will I get that need met?
- What kind of interactions do I need daily and from who?

Action:
Break it Down

For each aspect of care, brainstorm ideas for annual, monthly, weekly, and daily tasks.

Chapter Twenty-Three

IMPLEMENTING A CARE PLAN

In the past few chapters, we have walked through six different aspects of care: physical, emotional/psychological, professional, financial, spiritual, and social. We've brainstormed ideas that fit our preferences and needs, and we've strategically considered annual, monthly, weekly, and daily practices and habits.

You've also learned strategies throughout this book that could be included in your care plan.

If you find yourself struggling to come up with ideas, I encourage you to join the Teacher Care Network Support Community and see what other educators are doing. I have personally added several practices to my life based on ideas I've seen in the group.

Once you have a set of practices that you feel align with your wants and needs, it's time to bring it all together. I don't know about you, but I've made many lists and had many ideas in my life that never came to fruition. I had good intentions, but I didn't have a plan or a support system to help me follow through.

To help you follow through, consider breaking that list down into three types of care tasks and implementing them according to their type.

Interventions are care tasks and activities that may not be part of my routine, but when stress or upset strikes, I want to implement them to help me get back to a state of calm and rest.

TYPE 1: ROUTINES

Go through your list and identify tasks and activities that you'd like to do every single day. Most of these were probably daily or weekly ideas. Group together any tasks that occur in clusters.

For example, if you decide you want an "after school" routine for psychological detachment, that routine might include 1) threshold strategy, 2) 50/50 commute strategy, 3) decompress in the car for 5 minutes before going in the house. Your morning routine might include showering, packing a nutritious lunch, and eating breakfast.

Routines aren't things that we need to put in a calendar because they happen everyday. However, when we first start implementing a new routine, it's helpful to create reminders for ourselves. You might put a sticky note by the classroom exit to remind yourself to do the threshold strategy or a sticky note on your rearview mirror to remind you to do the 50/50 commute strategy. You might set an alarm on your phone for 30 minutes before you plan to leave for work to remind you to pack your lunch.

Once you've established the routine, you won't need as many reminders because the routine will have become a habit.

TYPE 2: SCHEDULED ACTIVITIES

There are some care tasks and activities that we don't do often enough for them to become routine, and some care tasks are not regularly occurring events. These might include doctor's appointments, meeting a friend for dinner, going grocery shopping, or spending time at a local lake to get out in nature.

For these care tasks, maintaining a calendar is crucial to implementation. I might have every intention of gardening this year as a way to care for my spiritual self, but if I don't put it on a calendar or set a reminder, implementation is at the mercy of my memory and the limited time available to me. By scheduling time on a calendar to engage in care, I prioritize the care task and increase the likelihood of actually engaging in the care.

Once you've identified your scheduled care tasks, take the time to enter them into your calendar.

TYPE 3: INTERVENTIONS

Interventions are care tasks and activities that may not be part of my routine, but when stress or upset strikes, I want to implement them to help me get back to a state of calm and rest. This might include breathing exercises, listening to a favorite song, doing a guided meditation, engaging in a practice of mindful self-compassion about something I did wrong, etc.

Once you've been doing interventions for yourself for a while, you might not need a list anymore. However, to get started, I find it helpful for clients to make a list of things they can do to care for themselves based on time increments. I recommend 30–60 seconds, 5-10 minutes, 15-20 minutes, and 30+ minutes. The list could be on an actual piece of paper that you keep in your desk or in a Note on your phone.

For example, if I sense stress and upset, and I have 10 minutes before my class comes back from lunch, I pull out my list, and on that list is a section that has practices that take 10 minutes or less. If it's my conference period, and I have 20 minutes, I can choose a practice that takes 20 minutes or less. If I'm standing in my classroom and the first bell is about to ring, I have practices I can do in less than 30 seconds.

Eventually you might not need the list, but in a time of stress, I find I can make a choice quicker when I have options in front of me.

Once you've identified routines, scheduled activities, and made your list of interventions, lean fully into scheduled activities and interventions, but roll your routines out one at a time. Scheduled activities are on a calendar, so they don't have to be remembered. Interventions occur when you're feeling upset, so you have a trigger to alert you to use them. Routines, however, will require the most effort and executive function to develop because they change how we go about living our lives.

Take your time. Don't drastically *increase* stress by implementing routines to *reduce* stress. Slowly walk in the direction of what you want to change, being mindful of why you're doing it, and embracing the support of your social support system.

Action:
Sort it Out

• Sort your care tasks into routines, scheduled activities, and interventions.
• Choose one routine to start integrating.
• Schedule your activities.
• Create a cheat-sheet for your interventions.

Chapter Twenty-Four

CLOSING THOUGHTS

Putting together a care plan and implementing new strategies will feel heavy for many teachers. The strategies and processes I've described are meant to be brainstormed, planned, and implemented over the course of weeks and sometimes months, depending on the person.

Change and healing is not meant to be done in days, or in one sitting. As someone who is a "doer" and understands what it's like to be the kind of person who just wants to get it done, I want to encourage you to take your time. Look at one section of the book at the time, one strategy at a time, one care area at a time. Get input and feedback from people who know you well and love you, and if you need further support join the Teacher Care Network Support Community or seek coaching.

There is a balance that I've been learning, even as I've written this book, between pushing yourself to be great, and giving yourself grace to be human.

This book is not about adding 50 care tasks and strategies to your to-do list so you can finally scream with resentment and resolve, "I AM TAKING CARE OF MYSELF!" This book is about choosing strategies and care tasks to integrate into your life that will enhance your life. This book is about choosing to take care of yourself in ways that will help you thrive the way you want. It is about choosing to live fully into your humanness.

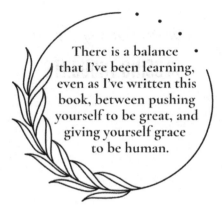

There is a balance that I've been learning, even as I've written this book, between pushing yourself to be great, and giving yourself grace to be human.

As I sat here thinking about how to close this book, I found myself staring out the window of my living room into my neighborhood, full of mature trees and older homes. I listened to the birds chirping and the rush of wind through huge pecan trees. I sat and stared and thought about you, the reader - the educator who would read my book.

I thought about the weight of the past few years.

I thought about the educators we lost in our communities from the pandemic.

I thought about the anxiety you feel about standardized testing.

I thought about the weight of school safety and the impact that has on your mental health.

I thought about the mandates you carry out with professionalism, even when you don't agree.

I thought about the days you've woken up and just didn't know if you could do it anymore.

I thought about your stress. Your tears. Your pain.

And then I thought about the hope I have for your future.

I wish for you, dear friend, a future where exhaustion, cynicism, and reduced professional efficacy aren't daily experiences - where burnout comes and goes, but doesn't make its home in your soul.

I wish for you a future where you can honestly say, "I'm okay," at the end of a long day of teaching.

I wish for you...

A future where you **Tend to yourself** and your needs in meaningful ways

A future where you **Harness social support** in ways that work for you

A future where you psychologically **Recharge through detachment** from work

A future where you **Ignite compassion satisfaction**

A future where you **Vow to honor your humanness**

A future where you truly THRIV™.

THANK YOU!

Thank you for spending your extremely valuable time and energy to read this book and give the THRIV™ process and concepts a try in your own life.

As a former teacher who values the process of learning, I appreciate the trust you've placed in me to guide you through the process of making sustainable changes, and I thank you for the honor of sharing my stories with you.

As an educational psychologist, I appreciate your consideration of the science that supports the strategies we learned.

As a mother and a member of the community, I thank you so much for the time you have spent and will continue to spend developing yourself so you can be the best teacher possible for the children you teach.

If you found any benefit here, please:

WRITE A REVIEW

Honest and heartfelt reviews keep me doing this work day after day as I advocate for fair treatment of educators.

Scan QR to leave a book review.

RECOMMEND

Recommend this book to a friend, to your principal, or to your school district.

MORE SUPPORT

Continue your journey at www.teachercarenetwork.com where you can:

- Access the **Teacher Care Network Support Community** full of free ideas and peer-to-peer support beyond what is included in the book.
- Connect with educators just like you who are slowly implementing changes and experiencing success.
- And SO MUCH MORE...

Always in your corner,
    Dr. Jen Johnson

RECOMMENDED RESOURCES

The Teacher Care Network™ Support Community provides a safe, free space for teachers to learn, discuss, and implement burnout prevention and recovery practices. Each potential group member is screened to ensure group safety to the maximum extent possible, so when you request to join, please answer the group membership questions.

Teacher Care Network™ Support Community:
www.teachercarenetwork.com/community

The THRIV™ Blog is a resource for teachers and administrators who are looking for short, relevant advice on a variety of topics related to the burnout recovery model, THRIV™.

THRIV™ Blog:
www.teachercarenetwork.com/blog

Dr. Johnson's THRIV™ Newsletter is an ongoing resource for teachers and administrators, and includes strategies and upcoming events that support educators as they implement their care plans.

Subscribe to the newsletter:

www.teachercarenetwork.com/subscribe

ACKNOWLEDGMENTS

My mom grew up in a home with an abusive mother. Her escape from the chaos and trauma was school, and the nurturers of her young heart were her teachers. Though she never graduated high school, she went on later in life to serve 6 years on the school board in City View Independent School District in Wichita Falls, Texas. She did this because she believed so deeply in the impact teachers make on the hearts and minds of children.

When I wanted to quit after the first two years of teaching due to the trauma I experienced, she said, "I support whatever decision you make, but I want to say this: You can leave the school system, but being a teacher is who you are. You couldn't escape it even if you wanted to." She was right, and the teacher I am deep in my soul is in large part due to her relentless advocacy for quality education for the kids on the "North side of the tracks" in my town.

Thank you mom, for the passion you built into my heart for K-12 education. Your legacy lives on in your absence, and you are dearly loved and missed.

Thank you to my husband, Marc, who is my biggest fan and the most amazing father to our son.

Thank you to my family, who have cheered me on and helped me take care of my son so that I could earn my PhD, run a business, and have the bandwidth to write this book.

To my academic mentors, Dr. Chad E. Smith and Dr. Melissa Savage: Each of you gave me skills, confidence, and support that made me into the professional I am today. Thank you to Dr. Cindy Froesch, who told me it was okay to not be a professor and to instead start the organization and be the support for parents and teachers that I wished existed. That "permission" changed my life.

Thank you to my coach, Dawn Nursick-Rubio, who has listened to my vision for the Teacher Care Network and continually helps me think through the logistics of making an impact. And to my executive assistant, Madison Venable, who helps keep me organized and moving forward.

Thank you to the beta readers, Mimi Rich, Adrienne MacIain, PhD, and my managing editor, Sierra Melcher, who helped me hone the message of this book.

To the Eleven - you make me who I am and I love you. To A and T - your love and acceptance have changed my life.

And finally, thank you to the teachers in the Teacher Care Network Support Community who authentically show up every week and vulnerably share their stories and their hearts with me and their peers. Your love for children and teaching inspire me to continue this work wholeheartedly.

REFERENCES

Alphabetical, by author:

Bakusic, J., Schaufeli, W., Claes, S., & Godderis, L. (2017). Stress, burnout and depression: A systematic review on DNA methylation mechanisms, *Journal of Psychosomatic Research, 92*, 34‑44.

Becker, L., Kaltenegger, H. C., Nowak, D., Rohleder, N., & Weigl, M. (2022). Differences in stress system (re-) activity between single and dual‑or multitasking in healthy adults: A systematic review and meta‑analysis: Physiological stress and multitasking. *Health Psychology Review*, (just‑accepted), 1‑45.

Bryant, F. B., Smart, C. M., & King, S. P. (2005). Using the past to enhance the present: Boosting happiness through positive reminiscence. *Journal of Happiness Studies, 6*(3), 227‑260.

Chen, C. C., & Petrick, J. F. (2013). Health and wellness benefits of travel experiences: A literature review. *Journal of Travel Research, 52*(6), 709‑719.

Cheung, Y. L., Lun, M. C., & Wang, H. J. (2022). Smartphone use after work mediates the link between organizational norm of connec‑

tivity and emotional exhaustion: Will workaholism make a difference?. *Stress and Health*, *38*(1), 130-139.

Cirillo, F. (2006). *The pomodoro technique (the pomodoro)*. Retrieved from https://www.infinityinc.us/wp-content/uploads/Pomodoro-Technique.pdf

Chung, T. Y., & Chen, Y. L. (2018). Exchanging social support on online teacher groups: Relation to teacher self-efficacy. *Telematics and Informatics*, *35*(5), 1542-1552.

Crum, A. J., Jamieson, J. P., & Akinola, M. (2020). Optimizing stress: An integrated intervention for regulating stress responses. *Emotion*, *20*(1), 120.

De Bloom, J., Geurts, S. A., & Kompier, M. A. (2012). Effects of short vacations, vacation activities and experiences on employee health and well-being. *Stress and Health*, *28*(4), 305-318.

Deci, E. L., & Ryan, R. M. (2000). The" what" and" why" of goal pursuits: Human needs and the self-determination of behavior. *Psychological Inquiry*, *11*(4), 227-268.

Erisman, S. M., & Roemer, L. (2010). A preliminary investigation of the effects of experimentally induced mindfulness on emotional responding to film clips. *Emotion*, *10*, 72–82.

Frost, R. L., & Rickwood, D. J. (2017). A systematic review of the mental health outcomes associated with Facebook use. *Computers in Human Behavior*, *76*, 576-600.

Germer, C., & Neff, K. (2019). Mindful self-compassion (MSC). In I. Ivtzan (Ed.). *Handbook of mindfulness-based programmes: Mindfulness interventions from education to health and therapy.* (pp. 357-67). New York, NY: Routledge.

Gilmour, J., Machin, T., Brownlow, C., & Jeffries, C. (2020). Facebook-based social support and health: A systematic review. *Psychology of Popular Media*, *9*(3), 328.

Gooding, A. D. (2003). Life coaching is not psychotherapy: There is a difference. *Annals of the American Psychotherapy Association*, *6*(3), 36-38.

Greenglass, E. R., Burke, R. J., & Konarski, R. (1997). The impact of social support on the development of burnout in teachers: Examination of a model. *Work & Stress*, *11*(3), 267-278.

Greenglass, E. R., Fiksenbaum, L., & Burke, R. J. (1996). Components of social support, buffering effects and burnout: Implications for psychological functioning. *Anxiety, Stress, and Coping, 9*(3), 185-197.

Komori, T. (2018). The relaxation effect of prolonged expiratory breathing. *Mental Illness, 10*(1), 6-7.

Lee, D. S., Orvell, A., Briskin, J., Shrapnell, T., Gelman, S. A., Ayduk, O., ... & Kross, E. (2020). When chatting about negative experiences helps—and when it hurts: Distinguishing adaptive versus maladaptive social support in computer-mediated communication. *Emotion, 20*(3), 368.

Luken, M., & Sammons, A. (2016). Systematic review of mindfulness practice for reducing job burnout. *The American Journal of Occupational Therapy, 70*(2), 1-10.

Maslach, C., & Leiter, M. P. (2017). Understanding burnout: New models. In C. L. Cooper & J. C. Quick (Eds.) *The handbook of stress and health: A guide to research and practice* (pp. 36–56). Wiley Blackwell.

Mellner, C. (2016). After-hours availability expectations, work-related smartphone use during leisure, and psychological detachment: The moderating role of boundary control. *International Journal of Workplace Health Management. 9*(2), 146-164.

McCann, L., & Pearlman, L. A. (1990). Vicarious traumatisation: A framework for understanding the psychological effects of working with victims. *Journal of Traumatic Stress, 3*, 131–149.

McKay, M., Fanning, P., & Ona, P. Z. (2011). *Mind and emotions: A universal treatment for emotional disorders.* New Harbinger Publications.

Pittman, T. S., & Zeigler, K. R. (2007). Basic human needs. In A. W. Kruglanski & E. T. Higgins (Eds.). *Social psychology: Handbook of basic principles* (pp. 473–489). The Guilford Press.

Preston, J. L., & Shin, F. (2017). Spiritual experiences evoke awe through the small self in both religious and non-religious individuals. *Journal of Experimental Social Psychology, 70*, 212-221.

Quoidbach, J., Berry, E. V., Hansenne, M., & Mikolajczak, M. (2010). Positive emotion regulation and well-being: Comparing the impact of eight savoring and dampening strategies. *Personality and Individual Differences, 49*(5), 368-373.

Sanchez, M., Haynes, A., Parada, J. C., & Demir, M. (2020). Friendship maintenance mediates the relationship between compassion for others and happiness. *Current Psychology*, *39*(2), 581-592.

Sias, P.M., & Bartoo, H. (2007). Friendship, social support, and health. In L. L'Abate (Ed.). *Low cost approaches to promote physical and mental health: Theory, research, and practice*. New York, NY: Springer Science

Sprang, G., Ford, J., Kerig, P., & Bride, B. (2019). Defining secondary traumatic stress and developing targeted assessments and interventions: Lessons learned from research and leading experts. *Traumatology*, *25*(2), 72.

Sun, J., Wang, X., Wang, Y., Du, X., & Zhang, C. (2019). The mediating effect of perceived social support on the relationship between mindfulness and burnout in special education teachers. *Journal of Community Psychology*, *47*(7), 1799-1809.

Turner, R. J., & Brown, R. L. (2010). *Social support and mental health: A handbook for the study of mental health; Social contexts, theories, and systems* (2nd ed.). New York, NY: Cambridge University Press.

Veerapa, E., Grandgenevre, P., El Fayoumi, M., Vinnac, B., Haelewyn, O., Szaffarczyk, S., ... & D'Hondt, F. (2020). Attentional bias towards negative stimuli in healthy individuals and the effects of trait anxiety. *Scientific Reports, 10*(1), 1-10.

Watkins, E. R., & Roberts, H. (2020). Reflecting on rumination: Consequences, causes, mechanisms and treatment of rumination. *Behaviour Research and Therapy*, *127*, 1-28.

Wendsche, J., and Lohmann-Haislah, A. (2017). A meta-analysis on antecedents and outcomes of detachment from work. *Frontiers in Psychology, 7*, 2072.

Wolkin, J. R. (2021). *Quick Calm: Easy meditations to short-circuit stress using mindfulness and neuroscience*. New Harbinger Publications.

Zarate, K., Maggin, D. M., & Passmore, A. (2019). Meta-analysis of mindfulness training on teacher well-being. *Psychology in the Schools, 56*(10), 1700-1715.

DR. JEN JOHNSON

Jennifer A. L. Johnson, Ph.D. (a.k.a. Dr. Jen Johnson) is an educational psychologist and the founder of the Teacher Care Network. Dr. Johnson worked in public schools for 10 years as an Interpreter, Deaf Education Teacher and Instructional Specialist in Special Education before working as a Teaching Fellow, Student Teaching Supervisor, and Research Assistant at the University of North Texas. She founded The Child Safety Collaborative, and subsequently the Teacher Care Network, to help schools address emotional health and safety concerns among students and staff through coaching, consulting, speaking, writing, and leading interactive workshops.

www.teachercarenetwork.com

 instagram.com/jenjohnsonphd
 linkedin.com/in/jenjohnsonphd

ABOUT THE PUBLISHER

Red Thread Publishing is an all-female publishing company on a mission to support 10,000 women to become successful published authors and thought leaders. Through the transformative work of writing & telling our stories we are not only changed as individuals, but we are also changing the global narrative & thus the world.

www.redthreadbooks.com

facebook.com/redthreadpublishing

instagram.com/redthreadbooks

Made in the USA
Monee, IL
05 January 2024

51000601R00089